Advance Praise for *Denial Is My Spiritua*

"Rachel G. Hackenberg and Martha Spong speak ...
and humor about 'denial' and 'failures of faith.' They give readers
a no-holds-barred presentation of their personal, interpersonal, and
professional struggles and losses. Through beautiful stories these
amazing women teach the reader how to move through denial and
failure into acceptance and grace. With insightful vision, they paint
a picture of life that prevails on the other side of failure using witty
and irreverent revelatory and profound stories. If you are searching
for honesty in the life of faith and how to live in the midst of struggles, this book will be a balm to your spirit."

—The Rev. Becca Stevens, founder of
Thistle Farms and author of *Love Heals*

"Disciplines of prayer and piety often feel far removed from the
grit of our daily lives. Yet, through these pages, Martha Spong and
Rachel Hackenberg are more than ministers; they become sisters on
a journey. With each chapter, they give us the gift of compassion on
ourselves, even in our darkest denials and in divine silences."

—The Rev. Carol Howard Merritt,
author of *Healing Spiritual Wounds: Reconnecting with
a Loving God after Experiencing a Hurtful Church*

"Rachel and Martha take a tremendous leap of vulnerability in
Denial Is My Spiritual Practice. In sharing their personal stories of
love and loss, they invite readers to participate with them as part-
ners in universal dance of making friends—or at least peace—with
both our light and our shadowy spaces. This book will resonate
with anyone who has ever learned the hard lesson that burying one's
head doesn't in fact make the hard thing go away. With thoughtful
personal narrative interwoven with biblical stories, *Denial Is My
Spiritual Practice* offers affirmation of the natural tendency toward

denial as a first response to hardship, while providing gentle nudges toward a new way of being in relationship with and not held captive by the valley experiences in our lives."

—Kentina Washington-Leapheart,
Director of Programs for Reproductive Justice
and Sexuality Education at the Religious Institute

"Spiritual practice takes many forms, and in *Denial Is My Spiritual Practice,* Rachel Hackenberg and Martha Spong share this essential truth. With insight, gasp-generating honesty, and wit, Hackenberg and Spong help readers appreciate how every event, every interaction, and every feeling can become an opportunity to learn more about living a spiritual life. Readers can expect to receive superb spiritual direction and practical pastoral care that will resonate well beyond one reading of *Denial Is My Spiritual Practice."*

—Meredith Gould, author of *Desperately Seeking
Spirituality: A Field Guide to Practice*

"Are you looking for brave companions as you delve into the inner life? In this lively, wise, and daring book, Martha and Rachel blend memoir, gentle humor, and biblical reflection to explore the experiences they never dared to discuss in church: bodies that fail, marriages that crumble, attractions that refuse to stay neatly contained. Throughout, they hold up the lens of scripture like a prism to reveal a spectrum of colors. Let this engaging book help you illuminate the beliefs that shape your life."

—Ruth Everhart, author of *Ruined and
Chasing the Divine in the Holy Land*

Denial Is MY SPIRITUAL practice.

(AND OTHER FAILURES OF FAITH)

RACHEL G. HACKENBERG
AND MARTHA SPONG

Church Publishing
NEW YORK

Church Publishing
19 East 34th Street
New York, NY 10016
www.churchpublishing.org

Cover design by Paul Soupiset
Typeset by Denise Hoff

Library of Congress Cataloging-in-Publication Data

A record of this book is available from the Library of Congress

ISBN-13: 978-1-64065-023-7 (pbk.)
ISBN-13: 978-1-64065-024-4 (ebook)

Printed in Canada

Ad gloriam Dei,
if such a thing is possible through failure.

CONTENTS

Denial Is My Spiritual Practice

Martha

I sat at my Baptist grandmother's Formica-topped kitchen table and watched her send carrots down the chute of her juice machine. Long slivers became bright orange juice in a glass. I asked to taste it. My four-year-old taste buds expected something sweet like the Tang the astronauts drank, with the velvety texture of the V-8 we bought in a big can. Instead it tasted like earth and went down like eraser crumbs. I did not ask to taste it again, but I did ask my mother why Grandma drank that awful-tasting stuff. I was a grown-up before I got the full answer. My grandmother was on a quest to improve her health, for reasons not merely medical but metaphysical. Her diet did not require carrot juice; rather, it excluded other things she liked. She viewed her ongoing gallbladder troubles as a warning from God. Her charismatic fervor for the juice machine matched her spiritual enthusiasm to figure out what God wanted from her and to offer it with all the energy she could muster.

The subtext of her efforts influenced my mother and, therefore, me. By generational osmosis I learned that ill health was explained by either blame or guilt—someone gave me a sickness through their sinful carelessness, or I caused it by my own sinful neglect of God's temple, my body. These theological understandings inclined us to a shamed silence about illness. Surely this prayerful woman knew more than we did. My grandmother left those she influenced with the impression that God's approval could be lost and won based on our own actions. I'm not claiming she disbelieved grace. I think she viewed her efforts as a significant supplement, just like the juice.

In my childhood, a polite silence about chronic health problems prevailed. Today, we live in the era of pharmaceutical advertisements promising to abate the symptoms of chronic illnesses. Happy people pack suitcases or fold laundry despite their rheumatoid arthritis (RA), play with their grandchildren thanks to help for their diabetic nerve pain, attend carnivals unafraid of their irritable bowel syndrome, and participate in outdoor activities even though they have lung cancer. Today, I see these short stories through the lens of my life with RA. In one television ad, a young woman sadly admires a pair of red high heels in a shop window, the implication being that she cannot wear those shoes due to her disease; RA can inflame or damage the little joints in our feet. Later, she leaves the store wearing the shoes, her life changed by an injectable biologic medication. These images treat chronic conditions as something curable, when the truth is that living with a chronic illness requires, for most patients, a lifelong commitment to self-care that does not always succeed at combatting the illness or its symptoms.

Growing up under my grandmother's influence left a mark, despite the contrary views I gained through my life experience, theological education, and spiritual discernment. In the back of my mind, in the depths of my heart, in the deepest recesses of my gut lingers a primal fear that I have done or am doing something wrong: a shame about being ill. A shame-based understanding of illness, or of any other bad things that happen in our lives, is fueled by the overriding narrative of popular Christian churches and groups based in the "prosperity" mindset. If we do things right, God will reward us. If we are suffering, God must be testing, or worse, punishing us.

My first symptom was a sore shoulder that wouldn't get better. I blamed it on shoveling the late February snow. My doctor sent me to a chiropractor, who rearranged me, gave me exercises, and then finally released me, saying he thought we had helped the shoulder, but there was still something; he just wasn't sure what. I remember he touched my hand and my wrist as he said it. I brushed it off. I believed I would get better.

A few weeks later, while attending a conference, I found I couldn't knit. My hands were sore, stiff, even swollen. My colleagues noticed the yarn and the needles sitting in my lap. My feet looked fat—well, fatter than usual—in my sandals. Shortly after returning home, I woke in the middle of the night and could not bend my fingers. The next morning, I had to call my twelve-year-old daughter to open the bedroom door because I could not turn the handle. That night my knee felt as though someone had driven a sword into it.

I called my primary care doctor again and began a journey through the medical system: back to her office, then down the hall to sports medicine for a check on my knees, out of that office to a physical therapist—the one who finally saw the symptoms and heard the history that made rheumatoid arthritis the most likely diagnosis. His mom had it, and he saw how the pieces went together. He sent me back to sports medicine, where the doctor spent more time telling me how sad her colleague in primary care was than she did asking how I felt. I'm a pastor, so I pastored her. There was no room for my feelings.

I'm not advising going to Dr. Google for advice, but when you look up RA (which some patient activists would rather we called rheumatoid disease), the first thing you see are the pictures of deformed joints. I wish I could say my concern was functional— could I knit? Hold a pencil? Fix dinner if the joints in my fingers went sideways?—but the truth is I didn't want my hands or feet to look like the pictures on the internet. My then-husband was away for an extended period when I got the news, but returned in time to go with me to meet the rheumatologist. I remember trying to explain why it mattered, when it seemed obvious to me that anyone hearing important information from an unfamiliar specialist ought to have a support person along. Why did that seem so mysterious? You find out in these moments what kind of person you're letting in close, who actually cares, and who only wants to be with you in good times. I remember sitting in a restaurant, crying, admitting my fear that I might not be able to do all the things everyone expected me to do and the things I loved to do.

"I don't want to be all taking and no giving," I said, in an odd quote of *9 to 5*.

I heard the reassuring answer, "You have given a lot, it's okay," but he would soon speak his truth: "I want to be a lover, not a nurse."

You find out who really cares about you when you are ill. A good friend became my best friend when she researched the illness and told me things I didn't know yet myself. An acquaintance living with RA became a dear friend and shared the Scripture that kept her going:

> Strengthen the weak hands,
>   and make firm the feeble knees.
> Say to those who are of a fearful heart,
>   "Be strong, do not fear!
> Here is your God.
>   He will come with vengeance,
> with terrible recompense.
>   He will come and save you."[1]

I wasn't exactly looking for vengeance, however. It was no one else's fault. There was no target for God's terrible recompense. That might have made it easier. The literature written for RA patients, who are mostly women, tended to be accusatory and was less than helpful. "Your joint fluid is attacking your joints," which seemed to mean, "Why are you hitting yourself, lady?" Instead, I hung onto the things my new rheumatologist told me, writing them down at home on Post-It notes and typing them into documents. The keys to living as well as possible with RA were:

- rest;
- exercise;
- medication;
- a positive attitude.

---

[1] Isaiah 35:3–4.

My body demanded rest. I am a type-A patient, so I took the medications. Exercise was harder—you're not supposed to overuse the joints that are inflamed. But the hardest thing of all was the attitude. While it is true that there are new medications, and there is a much lower likelihood of joint damage and deformities now, it's also true that the medications come with their own complexities because they suppress the immune system and make patients susceptible to infections, complicating recovery. Patients also face a higher risk of lymphoma, heart disease, and a depressing list of other complications, yet we are told we need to cultivate a positive attitude. Well. It's all fine when the medicine is working. When it stops working, the medical professionals describe it as the patient's failure, as in, "You've failed Enbrel." When another illness arises, you have to stop taking the RA medication; you get better from a cold or sinus infection while your RA gets worse. It can be hard to cultivate a positive attitude.

Denial is easier.

So I pretend I'm okay.

And I pretend, to myself, that I'm okay with it because I don't want to be one of those noble women who were bedridden or could not leave the house or were blind from birth, yet wrote the poems we find inspiring or the hymns we call classics. It's my worst nightmare. The times I have to stay in bed are also the times when I don't feel well enough to do much of anything useful, so I stream Netflix on my iPad. It does not cheer me up, as I usually conclude the world is a terrible place run by amoral villains like those on *Scandal*, or I am a terrible person for being in bed with the polygamous Mormons of *Big Love*.

If I felt good enough to write, it might help, as it has helped in so many other ways: making sense of things, providing a place to vent, or creating something beautiful that I think might help not just me but someone else, too. Most of my adult life, my spiritual practices have been grounded in words on paper—through journaling, making lists of people who need intercessory prayer, writing poem-prayers, studying in order to write liturgy, and preparing to preach.

I'm not drawn to more bodily practices. Yoga left me weeping, unable to contain the sadness I felt about my circumstances. You won't find me sitting on a prayer mat breathing, centering, and creating silence and space for God to do any talking to me. It scares me.

In my higher mind I believe that my grandmother was wrong, that God doesn't single us out for particular punishments to teach us certain spiritual lessons, but somewhere in my little Baptist girl heart lingered a fear that I did something wrong. I wasn't working hard enough or following faithfully enough. It's hard to imagine anyone else passing that harsh a judgment on my life, although I clearly exhibited atrocious taste in a partner at the time of my diagnosis. Otherwise, an examination of my life would have shown a woman in her forties working hard as a pastor and a mom, in the midst of an effort to get in shape that showed results in lost pounds and added strength. Things were going well for me, until suddenly they were not.

"Why me? Why now?" I wondered as I sat on the couch, hoping the medications would reduce the pain, the swelling, and the stiffness, and that I would once again be able to hold a pencil, or knitting needles, or a paring knife.

In the six months after the illness first flared, I suffered from prednisone-induced insomnia. I began to murmur the Serenity Prayer in the middle of the night. My twelve-step experience was limited to a few visits to Overeaters Anonymous, so I struggled to get the words right, but once I had them, I said the prayer again and again.

> God grant me the serenity
> to accept the things I cannot change;
> courage to change the things I can;
> and wisdom to know the difference.

My new mantra assuaged some of the desperation. By fall, the medicine was working, and the steroids had been withdrawn. I felt better. Aside from being sure to take the right pills on the right day, I felt (sort of) normal. I felt more comfortable putting aside the worries about my future health. When I listened to the parishioner who told me how her husband gave her RA injections, I separated myself from her problems. That would not be me, could not be me. My reflective and dependent period ended, and I went back to all giving and no taking, doing for others so they wouldn't have to do anything for me. The world supports denial. RA is an "invisible" illness, unless you reach the point where your joints are obviously deformed. A person has to know me pretty well, or be wise to the way rheumatoid disease presents, to catch on when I am not at my best. And I find when I let my discouragement show, I not only disappoint myself, but I also leave myself open to the unwelcome opinions of others—the people who can't see the illness, so they don't believe in it. I remember the winter day I was lying in bed with the kind of cold-bordering-on-pneumonia familiar to anyone who takes immune-suppressing medications. I scrolled Twitter on my iPhone, looking for news updates about the people occupying a wildlife refuge in Oregon. When I posted one of the stories on Facebook, a neighbor asked why I was wasting my time on the story. When I mentioned I was sick in bed and trying to amuse myself, instead of offering sympathy, she advised me to stop complaining.

Is it complaining to say how things really are? I remembered a long-ago Christmas, the first time I had seen most of my extended family since losing a baby midway through a pregnancy. My brother and his wife were coming with their infant son, a few weeks older than my son would have been, and I prepared myself for what I knew would be a hard visit. My aunt was coming to dinner on Christmas Day, an aunt who had lost a baby due to a tragic accident at birth. Even if no one else understood how I felt, she would. There would be an ally at the table. When she asked how I was, I told her. She shut me down.

"Don't you know that no one really wants to hear the answer to that question?"

Twenty-five years later, I continue to censor myself, to wonder if anyone else really wants to know how I am feeling, emotionally or physically. How can I be real with myself and keep from being real with others? If I can't trust the people who are family, friends, and neighbors for emotional support, I have to handle it all myself. That is hard when I'm feeling okay and even harder when I'm not.

Denial became my spiritual practice because, when I examined my situation honestly, I couldn't hold up the front of a positive attitude, even with myself. From day to day, it looks like this: whether I'm ill or relatively pain-free, I put my head down and do my work until I cannot. That is the great sin of my life over the past ten years, if we measure sin as those things that separate us from the love of God. If I sat to counsel someone living with a chronic diagnosis, I would encourage them to express all the feelings involved: fear, grief, even anger. In my own life, however, I resist the emotional work. When I let myself have my feelings, I'm afraid of the future, anxious that I will become a burden to my spouse or my children, worried that I already am. Instead, I keep myself as busy avoiding reality as my grandmother did with her juice machine.

As a pastor who is also a pastor's wife, I end up pretending I feel okay to two communities of faith. Recently I volunteered to help clean fingerprints off the pews at my spouse's church—a classic pastor's wife activity that almost no one nowadays would actually expect me to do. I arrived at church to find two much older ladies already at work, and I joined in, realizing to my dismay that getting up and down was much easier for these women twenty years my senior. Through extreme determination I kept at the task until we finished, instead of using an excuse that I needed to get back to other work, even though I did. That night, miserably stiff and sore, I confessed to my spouse something that came as a surprise only to me.

"I can't do what other people can do."

How can you have your real life if you can't confess to yourself or to God that you are ill and hurting? I can't do what other people can do. Denial denies me the consolation of a loving God.

Strengthen the weak hands,
   and make firm the feeble knees.
Say to those who are of a fearful heart,
   "Be strong, do not fear!
Here is your God.
   He will come with vengeance,
with terrible recompense.
   He will come and save you."

Maybe I need God to save me from myself.

You Should Feel This Pain

Rachel

T he x-ray shows that my neck has lost its curve. In black and white, I see the vertebrae stacked in a perfectly straight column, not at all the gentle slope from shoulder to skull that they're supposed to be.

"Without its natural curve," the chiropractor says, "your head feels like a hundred pounds weighing on your back, rather than ten. Your neck is at risk of slowly collapsing into an inverse curve." He clicks the keyboard and transitions to a new x-ray slide.

"This is your lower back." With a pencil tip, he draws short horizontal lines in the air in front of the image.

"Here. Here. Here. There should be visible disk space between each vertebra, but the space in your lower back is invisible to the x-ray. Long-term, without any change or help for your back, this will lead to a need for surgery." The chiropractor, who is several years younger than me and friendly almost to the point of informal, studies the image a moment longer and then turns to meets my eye.

"You're not in pain right now?"

I contemplate how to respond. Whether to tell him that I view the body as a tool in life, a mechanism for survival and purpose, the flesh that makes works-righteousness possible, the dust that will ultimately return to dust regardless of whether the time in between is luxurious or labored. Whether to tell him I have never given much credit (or much grace) to my flesh and its needs. Whether to observe—and how to observe, succinctly, rationally—that my internalization of others' disregard runs deep and thoroughly masks most manifestations of physical pain. Whether to say that it's perfectly normal for survivors of rape and abuse to experience disassociation from their own bodies. When, I wonder, is the appropriate moment in a doctor-patient relationship to tell your body's horror stories?

"No," I answer, short and sweet and true. "I don't feel pain right now."

I was thirty years old before I admitted to myself that I had been raped in college at the age of twenty-one. I didn't tell anyone else until I was nearly forty. That's ten years between the act of violence and the self-recognition of my own body's experience: literally a decade before I told myself the truth, and nearly two decades before I shared it.

Two decades ago, there was an early morning when I walked across the small grassy quad to my college apartment from his place in upperclassmen housing. A short but dazed walk around the common building in the middle of the quad, where we stored our bikes and schlepped our laundry baskets. I didn't bother to use the paved paths that were understood by most of us to be only suggestions for walkways. Back inside my apartment, my roommates gave me a hard, honest look and asked if I was okay. It was easier to respond with an upbeat, "I'm fine," than to say anything closer to the truth. And the truth was: I believed it was my own fault. I had said yes to going on a date with him—the movies at a nearby mall, who

knows what film we saw. I had said yes to going out for drinks after
we returned from the theater—I loved to go drinking and dancing,
and that night was no exception. I had said yes to returning to his
apartment to make out.

And then I had said no to sex. Repeatedly: no.

"You should feel this pain," the chiropractor said, but "should"
is a dubiously subjective word. Sometimes it's better not to feel
pain when your body isn't aroused for sex but someone else's body
is. Sometimes it's better not to register the shock that comes when
your "no" is so blatantly ignored. Sometimes it's better to hide your
soul far away when your body is intruded. Sometimes it's better to
pretend to be impartial toward your own experience—whether in
a bed, or on the street, or in a board room—any place where your
voice resigns itself to silence because its protest or its wisdom or its
creativity is so willfully and completely unheard. There are pains I
have preferred not to feel in life, even in the moments when they
were occurring. Instead, I have watched those experiences abstractly,
indifferently, with disconnected disgust.

Disgust is the right word. It was messy that night. I had my
period; he didn't care. I was bleeding everywhere; it didn't matter. I
tried to clean up afterward—my blood, his sweat—in the middle of
the night in a filthy college boys' apartment bathroom. When I had
done the best I could, I felt obligated to return to the bed and sleep
next to him for the remainder of the night as though nothing had
happened, as though it was just a date, as though it was perfectly
normal for him to have carried on without my consent.

"I'm fine."

"No, I don't feel this pain."

I've always admired Moses for that moment in the wilderness
when he stood over a dry dusty rock and told the truth about pain.[2]
On behalf of a community of people weary from generations of
enslavement and degradation, on behalf of people discouraged with

---

[2] Numbers 20:2–11.

their God's (in)ability to guide them swiftly to a promised land, Moses shouted to God.

"This hurts!"

On behalf of thirsty people tired of scrounging and begging for every drop of water, every crumb of bread, he cried: "My God, this hurts so much!" The years without hope—they hurt. The daily doubts—they hurt. The weary bodies, the parched tongues, the grumbling stomachs, the calloused feet—they hurt.

It hurts, God.

God, it hurts so much, but I can't admit it like Moses did. If I feel one pain, I fear that I will feel them all, and there are too many pains to feel and still function in any reasonable way. Yet there was Moses—not only functioning through pain, but admonishing the pain (and God) for its detraction from life. Moses, I have to imagine, was strained to capacity by the people's pain. He was tired of being the one who was always asked to know, to lead, to be strong. He was exhausted, too, by his own internal dialogue of self-doubt and God-doubt as each new day brought more wilderness, more wandering, more trying to get by, more unfulfilled promises. Against this back-drop of public pain, the incident at Meribah compounded a moment of Moses's personal grief—his sister Miriam had died.[3] Miriam, who affirmed God's work in Moses despite his years of living as a prince in Egypt, despite his years of living as a fugitive in Midian. Miriam, the leader who understood the on-the-ground movement for freedom while Moses negotiated for freedom in Pharaoh's highest courts. Miriam, the one who gave a song and a faith to the struggle, the one who was the backbone to Aaron's voice, the one who provided the personal touch in contrast to Moses's privileged face. Without Miriam, the wilderness threatened to be for Moses what it already was for the people following him: a meaningless waste, without poetry or beauty or wonder. And the dry rock represented it all: the grief, the doubt, the frustration, the impossibility of freedom.

"God, this loss hurts!"

---

[3] Numbers 20:1.

(thwack—the sound of a wooden staff against a stubborn rock)

"God, the people struggle!"

(crack—echoing against the far mountains)

"God, your promises are impossible!"

(smash—again and again)

"God, it's too much!"

The public protest of pain. The demand for God's promises. The insistence on life. The impulse to lash out at the Holy One from the depths of sorrow in our desperate attempt to provoke God's reaction and receive God's comfort. Moses gave voice and action to the words that I have always struggled to say: "It hurts." Yet common interpretation of Numbers 20:12 suppresses any such admission and admonishes Moses for his honesty of emotions. "He wasn't supposed to hit the rock *out of anger*," commentators write in an effort to explain why Moses's fulfillment of God's command to bring water from the rock could be interpreted as unfaithful. "His emotions were inappropriate. The wilderness wasn't *that bad*; Moses overreacted. If only Moses had trusted God, then God would not have been mad. If only he could have kept a cool head when the people expressed their doubts. If only he had not felt so raw after the death of Miriam. If only he had submitted to God, Moses would not have felt any pain at all."

It was Moses's own fault that he experienced pain, you see. Why didn't he cooperate with God? Why did he have to make such a big deal out of it?

The reporting of rape on college campuses is commonly discouraged, whether by the questioning tactics of campus police when victims dare to name their attackers, by the victim-blaming attitudes of peers, or by the suppressive actions of college administrations, among other measures. Beyond the campus, rape by a partner or spouse was not legally considered rape by U.S. laws until those laws began to change in the 1980s. Today, marital rape is still largely considered a "personal" matter, a domestic concern. Naming pain in a public space—especially the pain of sexual violence—is hushed for fear of

causing embarrassment and unease. Heaven forbid that you or I feel
awkward because someone voices their pain aloud, or that we find
ourselves ill-equipped to offer wisdom, unqualified to hear the hurt,
or imperfect to provide comfort and empathy. Heaven forbid we're
asked to be present to one another in difficult times, despite the weariness in our own lives. We prefer people to say that they are fine
when asked, otherwise how will we respond?

For as much as we do not know how to deal with others' pain,
many of us do not even know how to engage our own—especially
those of us who have experienced sexual violence and psychological
abuse. Too often we find ourselves following not in the footsteps
of Moses when he named pain in order to break open healing, but
rather in the mindset of those who interpret God as blaming Moses
for his emotional outburst and his gall in publicizing the pain. "You
should not feel this pain," we tell ourselves, "or at least, you should
not announce it for all the world to hear. Let our pain be buried in
the dust of the wilderness along with Miriam; we will wear our most
stoic faces and wait politely for God. Let our honesty of pain not
embarrass others or provoke God; we will trudge mutely through
the wilderness and ignore the blood on our calloused feet and in our
weary spirits."

What then should we say about Moses, his angry outburst of pain,
and his subsequent punishment from God? How else do we imagine
that he should have handled his pain in that moment? Upon receiving
instructions to bring water from a rock, should he have paused to
calm his feelings rather than striking the rock? Should he have gathered the people around that dusty rock and preached to them about
the cool refreshing fulfillment of prayer while they stood there, mouths
hot and parched? Would Moses have avoided God's punishment if he
had delayed God's reprieve of the people's pain by first satisfying God's
jealous need for their praise? Could the people's dis-ease with God have
been healed without the easing of their thirst? Could their doubts have
been answered if they were never named aloud? Can my back's tensions
be mended without confessing the memory of rape? Does the God who
loved us so much as to become flesh redeem humanity in spirit alone?

If we stand by a God who punishes Moses for his expression of anger and pain, are we implicitly upholding a requirement of silence for those who are injured? If we believe God tested Moses's patience in the face of despair, are we essentially declaring that those who seek justice must first genuflect to patience? If God cannot tolerate our outcries of pain, how can we expect compassion from one another or from ourselves?

God, this hurts!

Silence is no longer an option.

God, we hurt!

In mind, body and spirit—it is too much to bear alone.

God, this hurts!

Do not dismiss our cries.

God, I feel this pain. At long last, break open the dusty rocks of this wilderness and let a fresh stream flow without ceasing for the comfort of your daughter, for the relief of all your people.

High and Dry

Rachel

From a very young age I believed God did not hear my prayers: the magnitude of the world swallowed up in the holy vastness of God necessarily meant that my one individual voice could not be heard. And not just that it could not be heard, but that it did not matter if it was heard. I cannot remember a time when I did not believe this, quite matter-of-factly. It wasn't because God was dismissive or because my prayers were inconsequential but because God was really big and really busy. This was not a source of angst for me as a child; I was busy, too.

Although my prayer perspective would have several significant run-ins in later years with faith communities that believed otherwise, my childhood understanding was that prayer was less about relationship and more about my duty as a faithful Christian. My Sunday school teachers did not consider the question of prayer's reception to be a problem worth their attention. It was enough to emphasize the importance of prayer and to teach us the "Our Father" as we sat in the musty basement of our German Reformed church. The cement walls were painted in pale pastels, the floors were thinly carpeted, and our Sunday school classrooms were never quite warm enough in the winter. The basement-level toilets were always a frigid experience. We learned Bible stories on blue felt boards, made corresponding crafts, sang "Jesus Loves the Little Children," and said the Lord's Prayer before being dismissed from our short wooden chairs.

Excellence in prayer was not a hallmark of faithfulness in a congregation with a firm foundation in German stoicism. Nor was creativity. At church and at home, prayers were succinct: you knew what you had to say to God and you said it. There was no need to keep God waiting while you waxed loquacious all day. The pastor read brief prayers from the order of worship. The congregation's prayers were scripted into the liturgy. My father said grace each night at the family table, giving thanks and concluding with, "As we grow older, we pray that we might grow closer to you." This simple sentence remains one of my favorite prayers.

Despite the examples of brevity, when I tried to pray and make a connection to the Holy Vastness, I strove to make my prayers as big as possible. Every night I prayed for the whole world as thoroughly as I could: giving thanks for the unknown creatures in the wild depths of the seas, for the enormous whales and the swarms of tiny krill navigating the oceans' currents, for the dolphins that occasionally played near shore for the entertainment of beachgoers, for the tiny rainbow clams that burrowed and re-burrowed at the water's edge with every wave, for sand dunes and marsh grasses, for tide pools and fresh water streams, for rivers carving their way among hills and mountains, for cities and towns perched along those waterways, for the white-tailed deer that bounded through the forests and for the mountain goats that dared to live above the timberlines, for people across all longitudes and latitudes, and for rainclouds and hailstorms and thunder and snow. I prayed my thanksgivings topographically, on and on, night after night, putting myself to sleep long before my prayers could reach beyond the earth and into the galaxies.

Yet God remained out there, unreachable no matter how grand my prayers. The Wild Divine stayed decidedly inaccessible from the dust-to-dust confines of human flesh—or at least inaccessible from the particular dusty confines of my blonde, pony-tailed, tomboy flesh. Still, my grand prayers pleased and challenged me. God's distance was not a reason to be discouraged. I had plenty of meaningful rituals and responsibilities through my church and youth group (junior Sunday school superintendent, thank you very much) that shaped purposeful holy encounters. There was the rise and fall of

Sunday liturgy to convey the mystery of God. There were the words and tunes of hymns to carry the proximity of holiness into the heart. There were the classic youth group "talk about your faith in fun ways" activities to which I knew all the right answers. (Judas? *Bad*. Shadrach, Meshach, Abednego? *Aspirational*. Sex? *Never ever*.) If my prayers felt insufficient or ineffective, other habits of faith bolstered my spirit in ways that God would not.

High school and college interrupted my contented prayer life with the introduction of youth retreats and big-stadium Christian events. Those were the days of Amy Grant, Michael W. Smith, Petra, and *My God Wears Blue Jeans* (the actual title of a paperback devotional). That was a world of Christendom in which my childhood belief in an incomprehensibly holy God was deemed woefully irrelevant compared to the easygoing faith in which Jesus was your best bud, your salvific pal, your everyday walk-on-water Joe. If I had learned that prayer's answers were not to be sought because God's mystery was too great, in this drastically different theological world prayer was as easy as passing a note in class. There was no such thing as unanswered prayer because your BFF Jesus was right there, person-ally attentive to you, circling "yes" on your scribbled note of prayer, draping you with spiritual PDA.

I was startled by a world where people prayed with their hands in the air, sang with their hands in the air, and didn't seem to worry about their Sunday best. I couldn't fathom why I would want a God who dressed (literally or metaphorically or theologically) in blue jeans like me, or why I would believe in a God who was wrapped around my little finger like a boundary-lacking boyfriend. I didn't need a God who popped up a collar with eternal coolness. I needed a God who was God. (In hindsight, based on the popularity of churches across the theological spectrum whose goatee-sporting, jean-wearing, white male pastors still proclaim a hipster Jesus, I was clearly wrong about the importance of Cool Jesus.)

Given my experience of God's aloofness, it had never occurred to me that God might be a more personally intimate and emotional experience for others. I tried to fit into the prevailing Christian

culture, and by most measures, I succeeded. I was a small group
Bible study leader on teenage Christian retreats. I became president of my church youth group and then of my college InterVarsity
Christian Fellowship club. If I was puzzled by Cool Jesus, I appreciated that the people who crowded to him were genuinely pursuing
a meaningful connection to God, just as I was. We drew vastly different conclusions about what that connection looked like and how it
should be pursued, but I acclimated to the charismatic environment
and tucked my German stoicism into my back pocket.

I might have considered letting Cool Jesus put it into his back
pocket for safekeeping, but it remained stubbornly true that even the
most stylish blue jeans didn't make Jesus accessible to my prayers, a
point driven home painfully one day when a college student I did not
know asked me, "How has God spoken to you today?" The moment's
awkwardness was compounded by our context: we were standing at
the sinks in the middle of a church camp bathroom in upstate New
York. We were attending a retreat that brought together Christian
students from many different college campuses. I didn't know her
name, but there she was: challenging my experience of a distant God
like it was a normal bathroom topic, as though personal space had no
boundaries when it came to sharing faith experiences.

In one simple question, my contentment with God's silence was
deemed unworthy. I was *supposed* to be best friends with Jesus. We
were supposed to share *everything* in a constant stream of dialogue,
like girlfriends who never separated. My prayerful efforts to wrap
words around the vastness of God were clearly failures, and my
prayer life should have been ashamed of itself because it didn't result
in God's passionate whispers in my ear. My faith in a cosmic God
who knew the hairs on my head but didn't need to discuss them
with me in great detail unequivocally paled in comparison to the
friendship-bracelet-wearing Cool Jesus who, it should be noted, was
so intimately close with the other college students on the retreat that
he personally coordinated a few match-made-in-heaven dalliances.
When your college friends get the holy hook-up and you don't, you

start to wonder what's wrong with your spirit that God's voice isn't clear to you.

If my faith had been unimportant to me, I might have laughed it off and *tsk*ed the girl who scrutinized my relationship with God in the bathroom. Instead, like so many, I entered adulthood embarrassed to talk about personal prayer. I was skilled at corporate prayer, to be sure—a lifetime in the church hadn't left me without skills—but I avoided any spiritual sharing that risked the same judgment I had experienced in that unfortunate bathroom encounter. My negotiated distance with a mysterious God didn't cut it in a faith culture that valued an emotionally consuming Jesus. My unanswered prayers were a reason for discontent, an apparent indication that my spirit was dis-eased.

I was Leah in a religious culture that valued Rachel: Leah, the dutiful first wife of Jacob and the older sister of the beautiful Rachel, who was Jacob's second but favorite wife. Leah carried Jacob's children while Rachel carried Jacob's love. Leah's role in Jacob's life was utilitarian; Rachel's role was romantic. My faith wasn't pretty or inspirational. It didn't catch anyone's eye. It was useful that I could do the work of faith, that I was willing to labor continuously for Christendom, that I would pour myself into nurturing the spiritual life of others, but it didn't have the dramatic flair or charismatic spirit that could start a new church, or command a public pulpit, or prompt crowds to rush to the river for baptism. It still doesn't.

When you've been deemed useful but not worthy of affirmation, what else are you to do except continue to dedicate yourself to that very usefulness? What else could Leah have possibly done to elicit Jacob's affirmation? She poured herself into being useful to him, bearing first Reuben, then Simeon, Levi, and Judah, saying with each one, "Surely now my husband will love me."[1] In those ancient times, a woman's social worth was measured by the sons she bore; by those standards Leah excelled and should have been praised. Her whole body contributed to the prestige of Jacob's household. Still, he

---

[1] Genesis 29:32.

did not love her. She bartered with Rachel for his attention and gave birth to Issachar, Zebulun, and Dinah. Still, nothing. Fully half of Jacob's famed twelve sons came by the womb of Leah, and two more (Gad, Asher) by Leah's maid Zilpah, but he would not love her.

Leah nurtured and multiplied the life that Jacob had aspired to have since he first swindled the family inheritance from his older twin, Esau. She connived to spend time with Jacob, just as Jacob connived to increase his wealth. She dedicated years to bearing children, just as Jacob spent years working to earn Rachel's hand in marriage. But her usefulness never won Jacob's affection. She was as barren of love as her sister Rachel was barren of children. When Scripture was written over the centuries and Sunday school lessons taught to generations, Leah's faithful hard work was told as the backdrop to the inspiration of Rachel's beauty and the drama of her tears. There was no praise for Leah's many gifts of life, only lament for Rachel's death.

> Do not look in her eyes
> where dreams have died. Instead
> by her hips be gladly distracted;
> watch her hands—busy tending life.
>
> Where dreams have died, instead
> she has planted dogged resolve.
> Watch her hands—busy tending life
> in love's fruitless soil, barren of hope.
>
> She has planted dogged resolve
> by her hips. Be gladly distracted
> in love's fruitless soil. Barren of hope,
> do not look in her eyes.[2]

I put my prayers to use for the Church, determined to make myself useful before God. My stoicism might not garner God's affections,

---

[2] Rachel G. Hackenberg, "2 of 3: Leah," May 6, 2015, rachelhackenberg.com.

but surely my work ethic would save me. While God continued to evade me, I nurtured faith in others, offering tools for divine connection that didn't work for me: prayers for worship, prayers for books and blogs, prayer prompts for others seeking encouragement in their own prayer lives.

And still I wonder: How many prayers do I have to write for God to notice? How eloquent, how grandstanding, how beautiful, how emotional must they be for God to drop the veil of indifference and say, "I'm here"? How many ways can I write and name my lament over God's silence?

"Surely now God will notice me."

"Surely now God has heard me."

"Surely this time God will bless me."

"Surely this time I will return to praising the LORD."

Is prayer an act of barter, like Leah bartering with Rachel for extra nights with Jacob? Have I not yet met the price for God's attention? Is it a few mandrakes? A thousand prayers?

I continue to write. One prayer. Another. And another. I write a candid lament. I challenge myself to craft a soaring prayer of praise. I pen a shouting rejection of the God who turns away from Creation's pain and away from my own. I blog a prayer of solace that my heart longs to hear.

Even the most raging of my prayers are a beacon of hope: "Surely this time God has paid attention. Surely my usefulness will bring honor even to a struggling faith such as mine." The act of writing prayers becomes the answer itself. Even if they go unheard, they reflect my conviction that there is in fact a God before whom words are inadequate, a God whose wildness befuddles the most stoic and whose stillness unnerves the most charismatic, a God who is not obligated to the valuation of beauty or utility. Every prayer I write strives after such a God, and if God never hears my one individual voice within the vast mystery, at least I will know that I have spoken.

It's not even a prayer, O Wild Whisper. It's merely words strung together, bumbles of syllables and sounds, mutterings and half-finished thoughts, vain longings and (when I'm not careful) a snippet of heart truths that I prefer to keep to myself. I press on to meet you this way, to reach you this way, but what are nouns and verbs and punctuation compared to Life and Spirit? Of what usefulness are tongues, of what meaning are enunciations when all heaven sings your praises and every holy whim is more wise than my very best effort? Ah Sweet Mercy, bear to wade through my words and call me to the prudence of silence.[3]

The Point of Prayer

Martha

As a pastor, I am frequently asked to pray at events, especially before meals, even with my extended family. While some of my colleagues would just as soon be treated like civilians when they are not at church, I always say because I grew up Southern Baptist I can pray anywhere about anything. It feels more practical than pious. Praying out loud comes naturally after years of saying sentence prayers in Sunday school. The teacher would start the prayer, and we would go around the room. Sometimes we held hands, but regardless, there was a signal you could give to the person next to you if you

---

3 Rachel G. Hackenberg, "Prayer (Lent 27)," March 31, 2017, rachelhackenberg. com.

did not want to pray out loud. I never used the signal, and I learned which boys (almost always the boys) sitting next to me would inevitably use it, so I was ready when my turn came.

As a young student in an Episcopal school, I learned prayer book prayers. I am not sure I understood what we were praying about most of the time. I remember we prayed for "the President of the United States and all those in authority." I remember my mind wandering until, in third grade, I received my own prayer book to hold and read.

I often wander in prayer. Like a meditator struggling with monkey mind, I start in one place and end in another. Sometimes I just fall asleep. Whether in the early morning or at bedtime, I tell myself I will review the day or my hopes for it, and my mind goes for a walk instead.

At fifty, trying to figure out what the rest of my life might look like, I turned to the Episcopal order for Compline, praying Psalm 4 while lying in bed, hoping that the mildly obsessive repetition of the familiar words would soothe my agitation.

> Know that the LORD does wonders for the faithful;
>   when I call upon the LORD, he will hear me.
> Tremble, then, and do not sin;
>   speak to your heart in silence upon your bed.[4]

I created a companion list of intercessions containing the names of my loved ones and the family members who are harder to love, the leaders in the congregation I served, and others in need of particular prayer. I read the list a bit hurriedly at first, night-by-night slowing down to picture each person named. I remembered my Southern Baptist grandmother, considered a powerful pray-er by her friends, a faithful prayer group member, and the keeper of a significant prayer list. As a little girl, I spent the night at her apartment, sleeping in the

---

[4] Psalm 4:3–4, "An Order for Compline," *The Book of Common Prayer* (New York: The Church Hymnal Corporation, 1979), 128.

other high twin bed in her room. I remember watching her get the list out of her nightstand before I was old enough to read the names on it. When I was nine, I got a POW bracelet, meant to remind Americans of those missing or imprisoned in Viet Nam. While visiting my grandmother, I asked if she would pray for my missing soldier. She responded in strong terms: he was my responsibility; I needed to pray for him. She had enough names of her own. I was shocked, but empowered. Saying you will pray for someone should mean something. Otherwise, what was the point?

In that self-searching midlife time, I copied Compline and my prayer list into the Notes on my iPhone. Snuggled under the covers in a darkened room, I felt comforted, and, perhaps more importantly to me, I felt useful. My prayers could benefit others. I began to feel good about the discipline, which is probably the first sign that a spiritual practice is not working for us.

Several years ago, I attended a workshop to learn my Enneagram number. The Enneagram is an ancient system for self-understanding, used for many years by Roman Catholic spiritual directors as an aid in spiritual formation; in recent decades its use has spread through the Christian community and beyond. I found I was a 2, known as "The Helper." The teacher, Suzanne Stabile, took questions from the group, and someone asked about spiritual practices. I listened with interest, concern, and finally horror, as she explained that a 2 should not pray intercessory prayers. What? Some days my prayer list was the only way I could talk to God. Although I felt uncomfortable, I made myself listen. Helpers, she said, don't want to hurt people's feelings, so they say they will pray for everyone. When they can't manage to do it, they feel bad. You have to be serious about praying for someone if you say you will, she said. Don't say yes if you know you won't be able to commit to it.

I've felt that guilt too many times. I have meant well, but I haven't always followed through. The problem is magnified by our online connections. There is growing pressure to become part of the larger community of grief and outrage. We can't quit social media—well, we could, but it would be inconvenient. People from our workplaces, or our families, or our churches, use it to share things we need to know. We don't want to be that person who "doesn't do Facebook." So we play along. We give into the shorthand of contemporary syntax about prayer. We write "prayers ascending," although our cosmology really encompasses more than an up-down universe. We "send our prayers to," or claim "our prayers are with" a person who is grieving or suffering, even though people don't pray to each other. We write the words, but do we pray?

I suppose that fluttering my eyelashes heavenward while murmuring, even silently, a name or situation, may count for something, but what makes prayer work? Is it enough that my whispers help form the fringe of a thick blanket of prayers intended to comfort? Can my momentary focus on a bombing in the Middle East become one curve in a letter that composes an appeal to the Almighty to have mercy on the bereaved and the terrified? Maybe I am kidding myself to think anything I do helps in a distant situation. Worse, perhaps I am getting myself into trouble, like the Pharisee in a story Jesus told.

> He also told this parable to some who trusted in themselves that they were righteous and regarded others with contempt: "Two men went up to the temple to pray, one a Pharisee and the other a tax collector. The Pharisee, standing by himself, was praying thus, 'God, I thank you that I am not like other people: thieves, rogues, adulterers, or even like this tax collector. I fast twice a week; I give a tenth of all my income.' But the tax collector, standing far off, would not even look up to heaven, but was beating his breast and saying, 'God, be merciful to me, a sinner!' I tell you, this man went down to his home justified rather than the other; for all who exalt themselves will be humbled, but all who humble themselves will be exalted."[5]

---

[5] Luke 18:9–14.

Social media tends to make us all feel like we have an important platform for making proclamations on events and ideas. Maybe you have those friends who always share the latest take on a current news story. Maybe you also have one who offers some spiritual interpretation, and another who calls us all to pray, and yet another who exhorts us to remember that prayer is not enough—we need to act.

Look, Lord: I am not like other people who use social media only to read about the latest pregnancy in the Duggar clan. Not I. When I see a sad story, I share it and offer up words like, "Please pray for the lost and forlorn people who suffered a terrible tragedy." I choose my words carefully, for maximum effect. Sometimes I even scold people I presume are not praying properly. I am so pious.

Um, no. Please stop, self.

At times, my prayer practice dwindled. I continued to write prayers for work and worship. I still tossed the over-the-shoulder prayers we utter when we're harried. I certainly prayed with fervor while taxiing to the runway on every airplane ever. As I worked through my internal struggle, I named a lack: I missed praying with other people. Praying alone felt lonely.

When the opportunity came to start a church prayer group, I welcomed it. Not all praying with others is good, however. If you have ever noticed who gets the e-mails or calls that go out to a church prayer chain, you might suspect that some people are in it for the fresh news of injury, illness, breakdown, or death. When I suggested our group could spend significant time in silent prayer, I faced a rebellion. Members preferred spending group time discussing their own difficulties and getting updates on the sick and the troubled folk on their lists. My idea of spending time in prayer together was different, less interesting, and probably harder. Well, definitely harder.

I confess, my ideal for prayer in such circumstances is the same ideal I find difficult to explore in my own prayer life. I want words I can rely on, not silence that might be filled by some force other than my own will. I understand the concept of meditation or centering prayer as an emptying that makes room for the Spirit of God. We can't know, when we stop talking and start listening, whether God will console us, call us, or caution us. My conclusion, based on other moments of communication with God, is that whatever happens, it won't be what we thought we needed. Perhaps that is part of my resistance. There is surely a thread connecting my embrace of studying and writing and praying with others over and against simply sitting and listening. I excuse it this way: it's my calling to help others, to be present to them, even to enable their spiritual experiences. Somehow that does not extend to my own self.

The times I have tried to make meditation or silent prayer part of my practice have shown me how geared my routine is to the needs of others. As a young mom, I signed up for a class at church that involved the homework of contemplative time, with the encouragement for the work of centering prayer to be done early in the morning. I began waking up before my family, but no matter how early I got up, my baby woke up, too. It was years later before I realized that the sun was hitting his window earlier each day of the twelve weeks the class met.

It was easy to say to myself, "That is just not for me. My life does not allow the time for it." Contemplative prayer became a goal for retirement, like learning how to hand-spin yarn or how to quilt. I continued to respond to the needs of others, whether in the literal sense of raising young children or in the more emotional territory of being a friend and, later, a pastor. My characteristic of caring was so well known that, once during college, a friend hung a sign on my Ford Pinto, naming it the Mobile Crisis Unit. It's possible that the friends I picked up and took out for pizza received some benefit from their rides in the Pinto, that they felt heard and known, but the truth is I got a lot of satisfaction from feeling needed. I also managed to ignore things that mattered for me but were painful to recognize, including my lack of a plan for life, my heartbreak over the end of a relationship, and the other things that ran deeper but were not acknowledged until many years later. Caring about friends and focusing on their problems was easier. As the caregiver of the community, I had an identity.

There is nothing wrong with taking care of people who need it. Parents and grandparents do it; at midlife we may begin to care for our parents, or find ourselves part of the "sandwich" generation. Friends lean on each other. We all need the people who work in helping professions. Taking care of others is good, when it is our responsibility. Maybe it's the same with prayer.

When my mother was dying, she did not want to admit the diagnosis of metastatic melanoma, even to her closest friends. Undeterred by her silence, three ladies decided to pray for her at the same time every morning, and they invited me to join them. Their intention was that she be well again. She was sixty-seven; they could not bear to think she might die. The doctor gave a clear prognosis: She might have four to six months. I was scared to lose my mother, but I was sure she was going to die. She believed illness came as punishment and wondered what she had done wrong. I did not pray for a cure, but asked for her healing. I prayed for her peace. I prayed that she would stop blaming herself.

The way those prayers worked surprised me. My mother came to a place of readiness for whatever might be waiting and I felt closer to her than I ever had. Instead of straining to be her daughter in the "right" way at the end, or waiting for permission to do what someone else expected, I showed up and breathed through the last days with my parents. At her bedside I played a cassette given to her by a family friend, a recording from the Taizé community. Mother loved the setting of the thief's plea, "Jesus, remember me when you come into your kingdom."[6] We listened to that one again and again, joined in prayer with the rising voices on the tape.

What is the point of prayer? There have been times in my life when my needs were so apparent that friends could not avoid seeing them. In the middle of a hard night of relationship and soul, I reached out by e-mail to friends around the world, asking for help. They stepped up, these friends, these women of faith, these angels in a night slow to end and the morning that succeeded it. They

---
[6] Luke 23:42.

prayed for me when I could not pray. When I grew so numb from lack of sleep that I could feel nothing else, I felt their prayers spinning a web of love and hope and sincere concern so strong no loss could break it. I knew I was not alone. I learned just how prayer deepens our relationships with God and each other. It only came about because other people prayed for me.

For a long time the only thing I could remember about what Suzanne said was that Helpers should not pray intercessory prayers. What she meant was we shouldn't only pray for others. List making and name reciting leaves little space for the work we can do in prayer and the work prayer does on us. Our two-way relationship with God must be the point of prayer.

When others tell me a right way to pray, I still bridle. I hope and trust that there are as many kinds of prayer that work as there are people. For me, writing seems to be the way to express what I hope God will hear. I write prayers the way I write most things, looking for the intersection between God's word and life in the real world. Somehow the process opens the door for me to a sense of God's presence.

When it comes to a daily practice of meditation, I remain a failure. I cannot seem to make that perfect space and time that contemplation suggests to me; I do not have the proper chair or cushion, or live in a house that provides space for a home altar or prayer corner; I do not find it easy to form the intention to be in silence. I do, however, spend a fair amount of time at my desk staring out the window at a Japanese maple tree, the last in the neighborhood to drop its leaves. The dry brown bits and the bare ends of the branches quiver in the mid-winter breeze. They blur before me, and my mind gets quiet, and I am not so self-conscious about the process. Then, things happen. Words get through. Stuck ideas shift.

But the tax collector, standing far off, would not
even look up to heaven, but was beating his breast
and saying, 'God, be merciful to me, a sinner!'[7]

I hope that even though I am sharing this prayer with you and God
in public, I am offering it with all humility.

Lord,
I'm pretty clear about my limits.
I lose the thread of the conversation
    when I pray at bedtime.
I doze off.
I pray in the car, but I keep my eyes open.
I know I should pray first thing in the morning,
but,
my mind goes right to work.
I struggle to find the quiet for contemplation.
(I hope contemplating trees counts.)

I can only bring you myself,
with my busy mind,
and my will to work,
and hope you can do something with me.
I trust you can, trust you will have mercy on me.
Otherwise, what's the point?
Amen.

---

[7] Luke 18:13.

3 · HONOR YOUR FATHER AND MOTHER

Spare the Rod

Martha

M y mother had slender hands with the long, elegant fingers of a gentlewoman, but they stung when she spanked me. She parented in the manner of her generation, and her parents' generation, and it left me with a certain impression about the parenting of God. We had best avoid God's wrath, because the punishment would hurt even more.

The knowledge I have about my mother's childhood is mostly mythical. She died in 1993, so I cannot fact-check my memories. I can only say what I gathered from my experience of her and how it formed me. I know others perceived her as kind and gentle; she saved her occasional sarcasm for private settings. She grew up in a Marine Corps family. Her father rose to the rank of brigadier general. She used her hands creatively and constructively for many things. She was a wonderful gardener, an accomplished seamstress, a competent knitter, and a precise gift-wrapper. While my father lived the life of the mind, she made sure the household ran smoothly, attending to oil changes, lawn mowing, hiring help and repair men. She never called on him for a domestic task beyond his claimed capabilities: hanging pictures, mixing cocktails, and laying a fire. I don't know anyone else who ever saw her angry.

I was not a perfect child. I spent a lot of time waiting outside the office of the head of the lower and middle schools at St. Agnes, my Episcopal girls' school. I was often scolded by the giantess who held that lofty position. In second grade, I brought home old school punishments, condemned to write out a hundred times, "I will not talk while Mrs. Barber is talking," or "I will not stomp in the hall." My guess is I did plenty of things the adults in my life found smackworthy. According to the parenting practiced in the American South of my childhood, physical punishment of a child raised no moral quandaries. After all, it wasn't just cultural; it was biblical.

> Those who spare the rod hate their children,
> but those who love them are diligent to
>   discipline them.[1]

Spare the rod, and you spoil the child. Smack a bottom or a hand, and you do right by that child; you teach them to behave well and to be safe. To substitute a hand for a rod—or a belt, or a switch, or a paddle, or a wooden spoon, or a ruler—seemed civilized.

My mother, who had a degree in social work from Cornell University, relied on Dr. Spock, who tried to turn parents away from physical punishment and the rigid practices accepted before World War II. I infer from her parenting style and choice of discipline that the idea of spanking as a punishment was baked into her. She once told me, using a phrase many others have, "Never spank in anger." Here, she disagreed with the good doctor, who thought as I do. I find it hard to imagine any feeling other than anger that would inspire me to strike another person. How cold would a person have to be to wallop a child in order to make a point after the moment of passionate response has gone by?

When I say I was gently raised, I mean, in part, that I learned genteel manners from both my parents, but I think first of my father. He was authoritative, though rarely angry; kind, though not particularly warm; serious and humorous, both. My father never laid a hand on me. I don't think of him as particularly embodied, to be honest. He spent most of my lifetime thinking great thoughts, too busy with the important work of politics and law to come down to earth with

---

[1] Proverbs 13:24.

the rest of us. After my mother's death, he made a fairy tale out of their marriage, claiming to have rescued her from the home she had with her parents.

The greatest moments of tension I remember between the two of them related to my brother, who got into the kinds of trouble that relatively well-off white boys can without risking their future. I remember my mother calling on my father to be the disciplinarian, and he was angry enough in some of those moments to bring down the wrath of heaven and hell together on that teenage head. At least that's what I remember from the other side of the door or wall, or from the top of the staircase, removed and safe.

Everyone in the house knew when these scenes unfolded, but the dramas my mother and I acted out belonged only to us. I remember them like dreams; did that really happen? I remember them like documentaries; the facts are clear. I remember them in IMAX; the world shakes and rolls. I was seven and lit matches with my brother. I tried to escape the punishment, but she caught me. I was nine and talked back. By then, I knew to hide in the powder room until she cooled off. I was eleven and gave her a look of disdain. She slapped me across the face. I learned that when we make people angry, or when we disappoint them, they will lash out at us. I learned that being angry gives us permission to lash out at others. There is just enough evidence of this kind of thing in the Bible to put the actual fear of God into a child. If our disappointment and anger at another person allow us to strike a blow, God's wrath becomes terrifying.

I grew up and went to theological school and gained a more sophisticated understanding of the Trinity, that Father and Son and Holy Spirit are all one, yet I still sometimes fall into my childish understanding, thinking of Jesus as the friendly one who loves me, the Spirit as the static electricity making things happen in the world, and God-the-Father-Mother-Parent as the one who views me as a disappointing example of humanity and would just as soon smack me as look at me. The things I learned, the impressions I received, the handprints I felt all remain with me.

I did not become a professional good girl overnight, but clarity helped. When I was a teenager, the rules for behavior expanded beyond manners and respect for moral codes. Avoid the holy smackdown—do not smoke, do not drink, do not do drugs, do not have sex, especially do not get pregnant before getting married—and all will be well. Up on the second floor of the Court Street Baptist Church, the junior and senior high Sunday school class built a loft for youth group meetings. The huge project involved taking down a wall and a ceiling, bracing a platform, and making a gigantic mess intended to show that the church really cared about its young people, and, more particularly, to show a new family in the church that, in 1973, we were open to new ideas. Underneath the construction, in a room that would never be free of cinder block dust, we had our more formal class on Sunday mornings. We checked ourselves off in the attendance book: "Present," "Offering Brought," "Bible Read Daily." Then, with the bright summer sun pouring through the windows, we opened our Bibles.

> Now all the tax collectors and sinners were coming near to listen to him. And the Pharisees and the scribes were grumbling and saying, "This fellow welcomes sinners and eats with them."
>
> So he told them this parable: "Which one of you, having a hundred sheep and losing one of them, does not leave the ninety-nine in the wilderness and go after the one that is lost until he finds it? When he has found it, he lays it on his shoulders and rejoices. And when he comes home, he calls together his friends and neighbors, saying to them, 'Rejoice with me, for I have found my sheep that was lost.' Just so, I tell you, there will be more joy in heaven over one sinner who repents than over ninety-nine righteous persons who need no repentance."[2]

---

[2] Luke 15:1–7.

It was the minister's daughter, a little older than I, who angrily challenged our teacher, asking, "Doesn't God care about the ninety-nine who stayed out of trouble?" For good girls who tried to be the best at being good, was there no reward? Why did Jesus care more about the runaway? I considered the prayer I had learned in Episcopal elementary school.

> Almighty and most merciful Father,
> we have erred and strayed from thy ways
> like lost sheep . . . .[3]

Those sheep were in trouble. Using the wisdom of the proverb, a straying sheep should have been punished, not celebrated. Spare the rod, spoil the sheep. I remember sitting quietly, trying not to let my rising eyebrows be visible to the teachers. Could you really be that angry with adults, right to their faces? Was the minister's daughter going to get into trouble? I agreed with her idea, but wasn't she running off with the class as surely as the one ran off from the flock of ninety-nine? It was hard work to be good all the time, especially if the Bible said God cared even more about the ones who were not.

I entered adulthood and became a parent, still unsure where I stood on misbehavior and divine punishment, but pretty sure I had been good, or good enough. I could count on one hand the times I had done some drinking in college, or had held a cigarette when friends smoked, but otherwise, I had stuck to the rules. Then I had a baby who quickly became a toddler, with the interests a toddler will have, which included a drive to explore electric sockets and a desire not to do what his parents expected. I felt less conflicted about slapping a little hand away from danger than I did the petty smacks issued to bring an independent spirit into line. There had to be something other than inspiration by fear in the parenting playbook. My oldest son, Edward, in his toddler wisdom, seemed to see things the

---

[3] Daily Morning Prayer, Rite One, *The Book of Common Prayer* (New York: Seabury: 1979), 41.

same way, piping up during a major snowsuit struggle with his father, "Why hit me, Daddy?"

Both my husband and I had grown up being spanked. We needed to find a different way to do things because neither of us felt good about our little one's rebuke. My copy of James Dobson's *Dare to Discipline* warned me that if I did not discipline my son, the courts would have to do it for me. Confused, and willing to be converted, I confided in a mother with older children who expressed shock that we would ever spank. By the late 1980s in New England, where we had moved with our little son, educated parents who struggled to get their toddlers into weather-appropriate gear employed other models of parenting.

We tried, reading Rudolf Dreikurs[4] instead of Dobson, teaching natural and logical consequences instead of exerting our authority for the sake of being in command. By the time Edward turned four, he had learned all the consequences and thought he could employ his own logic to reason his way out of them. Picture a tired, pregnant mother attempting to stop a behavior she found frustrating by banning a favorite TV show.

"Edward, if you do that one more time, you will lose your *Ninja Turtles* privileges for a week."

He pondered for a moment and replied, "Oh, Mommy. Couldn't you just spank me? You don't hit very hard."

That story became such a strong thread in the fabric of our family life that his then not-yet-born younger brother is convinced it happened to him instead.

As I vacillated between Dobson and Dreikurs, my mother sent me a book written by Kitty Kersey, the wife of my childhood minister and the mother of my Sunday school classmate. As Mrs. Kersey, she was the founder of the first school I attended, a church preschool and kindergarten. She was my absolute idol. As Dr. Katharine Kersey, she had a career in early childhood education and development,

---

[4] *Children: The Challenge* (New York: Dutton Adult, 1987), and other editions in reprint.

teaching at Old Dominion University, writing textbooks for teachers and guides for parents like the one my mother put in the mail. *The Art of Sensitive Parenting* offered alternatives to physical punishment, calling on the hearts of parents. As a mother, I felt a sense of relief; as a daughter I felt a little jealous of my old Sunday school classmate. What was it like to have a mother so gentle that she would never think of spanking you? Maybe it gave you the courage to speak up, to ask the questions no one else would ask, to expect your ideas and beliefs to be acceptable.

My hand is not like my mother's. My skin is rougher, less lady-like, but my plump palms and short fingers are softer. Even after the Snowsuit Awakening and the Ninja Turtle Throwdown, there were times I delivered a smack on a bottom. I know Edward was right about how hard I hit, but I was just as much out of control when I hit my children as my mother ever was. Now I understand the problem with my childhood conclusions about God's wrath. God is not human. We can trust God not to lose her mind and lash out at us, not to use his mighty hand to wreak havoc. I'm convinced that most of the Bible stories about God's anger with Israel grew out of a need for an explanation for losing a war, or suffering through a famine or a plague or a drought. God is far too busy looking for the lost sheep to be plotting punishments for ordinary sinners. That seems to apply to extraordinary sinners as well.

> . . . we have left undone those things which we ought to have done, and we have done those things which we ought not to have done.[5]

I tried to learn a more excellent way to be a mom, yet I made my own mistakes. Maybe that was inevitable. We try to do it differently and come up with new ways of doing it wrong. I let my children think if they pursued their interests that all would be well. Then the economy took a downturn just as they reached adulthood. When he

---

[5] BCP (1979), 41.

turned thirty, I apologized to Edward for predicting a future of abundance that did not materialize. He responded with a wry expression, "It's okay, Mom. That was the nineties."

Such mercy and good humor, where did he learn it? Maybe I did some things right, some of the time. When I felt that angry God coming to life in my head, I bit my tongue. I took a breath. I wanted my children to know God differently. Surely God, who is merciful, does not want to frighten us into submission. Surely God, who is loving, wants us to do right in response to that love.

> But thou, O Lord, have mercy upon us,
> spare thou those who confess their faults,
> restore thou those who are penitent,
> according to thy promises declared unto mankind
> in Christ Jesus our Lord.[6]

Surely God didn't put God's own self on the line to scare us. If God had wanted to do that, Jesus could have come riding a horse and swinging a sword, or in a uniform with medals across his chest, deploying his troops, employing the rod.

My mother has been gone a long time; she died in 1993. She knew two of my children, but only the oldest has any memories of her. Most of what they know about her comes from me. While working through my own past, I said too many things about her mistakes. One day a teenaged Edward replied, with a touch of malice, "Grandmommy was not a very nice lady."

I regret my willingness to punish my mother in my memory the same way she punished me in life: as a reflex in moments of anger or unhappiness. I also remember the way she taught me to bathe Edward, her quiet support when I had trouble breastfeeding him, the checks she sent when our household did not have enough money to go around. I see her playing at the kitchen table, or on the beach. I see her patience as Edward told her the names and personalities

---

[6] BCP (1979), 41.

of all the Ninja Turtles and their associates and even the bad guys, Bebop and Rocksteady, who, he told us, "came over to the Good." I remember her hands touching my new baby's feet. Peter, she said, had "the feet of a dancer." They both danced, those boys, but she never saw it. She was gone before Edward acted in his first play, when Peter's only musical instrument was a frying pan played with a wooden spoon, in the long ago when we had not imagined Lucy.

This is not to say my mother should not be held accountable for the things she did and the lessons she taught. It is to say, I'm accountable, too. I wish I had portrayed her differently to my children. I wish I had been merciful. I talk about her differently now, perhaps because I wonder how they will talk about their own mother. I hope someday they will see how complicated we all are, how complex working through the things that happen to us in life can be. I hope they will choose to spare the rod, not just for her, but for me.

Silence in the Sanctuary

Rachel

When I turned five, I was no longer allowed to play in the nursery during Sunday morning worship. Five was a magic number: a threshold of maturity. The onset of kindergarten meant my parents considered me old enough to sit quietly through worship in church. I felt confident that I was old enough, too, although I wondered who would be left in the nursery to neatly organize the plastic cows and the lone brown horse in the nursery's Fisher Price barn, who would find the missing puzzle pieces when it was time to clean up, and who would organize the toy shelves appropriately: every cloth book with its fabric pages lying flat; the dolls sitting together in the cribs, skirts smoothed to protect their decency; the plastic pianos and xylophones lined up with keyboards in the same direction; and the small wooden chairs pushed in around the white linoleum coloring table. It was hard to believe that any other child would live up to that standard of nursery order now that I had graduated to the sanctuary.

But dutifully I went to worship and sat still, feet dangling from the hard wooden pew, legs too short to reach the carpeted floor. Without the happy nursery time to order and reorder toys, I became fascinated by the orderliness of worship. The acolyte and choir processed, somber, serious, prayerful in their green robes, with the pastor at the end of the line in his flowing black robe. Familiar opening words every Sunday cloaked us with the presence of grace:

> In the name of the Father, and of the Son, and of
> the Holy Spirit.[7]

The Trinity was the very compulsion for our worship, the authority that called us together as church, the holy relationship by which we organized our lives. An invocation and opening hymn united our voices:

> Holy, holy, holy . . . .

The confessional prayer followed, because we could only come before the God Above All Gods with utter humility and bare honesty:

> We have grievously sinned against thee in thought,
> in word, and in deed. Pardon our sins, take away
> our guilt, and grant us thy peace. (*Ah, the sweet
> poetry of thee's and thou's.*)

---

[7] Excerpted liturgies from *The Hymnal* (Eden Publishing House: Saint Louis, MO, 1941.)

The subsequent assurance of our pardon:

> Hearken now unto the comforting assurance of the
> grace of God . . . . (*Can we please return "hearken"*
> *to our modern vocabulary? I'd like to have my GPS*
> *programmed to say, "Hearken now, turn left at the*
> *Starbucks and continue for two miles."*)

Every Sunday, we offered the same *Praise ye the LORD* and sang *Glory be to the Father* from the back pages of the hymnal. Every Sunday, the words of Scripture were intoned from the lectern. There was no newfangled political correctness. We only had "men" in our pew Bibles. Every Sunday, the children's time was a primer in Christology: Follow Jesus. Love Jesus. Remember Jesus died for you. On special occasions, there was a candy treat from the pastor after we recited the Lord's Prayer.

The congregation sang a second hymn, a holy sound that masked the pounding feet of children returning to their pews or, for the fortunate ones, to the nursery for the second half of worship. For a young girl dangling her feet in the pew, the pastor's sermon was a time to solve the puzzles in the children's bulletin. These were easy entertainment—the fill-in-the-blank Scripture puzzle was not very puzzling, the hidden object was never hard to find, and the word search was accomplished quickly—so they didn't always guarantee my obedient stillness. Thankfully, the pastor's sermon rarely ventured beyond ten minutes.

Prayer time was just as well-mannered as the rest of worship, with folks standing in turn to name those in need of prayer. The pastor alone had the authority to bring those names before the altar:

> for George, for Agnes, for Ralph, for Joyce, for
> Mildred, for Arthur.

There were announcements, too, highlighting acts of faithfulness through rummage sales and CROP walks. We stood and recited the

Apostles' Creed; I would have to wait until later years to discover the poetic beauty of the Nicene Creed. We sat again to pass the offering plates—our humble effort to show God that we did not ask for handouts, but came to faith and life ready to do our fair share:

We give Thee but Thine own.

We sang one final hymn and then the bells chimed as choir, pastor, and acolyte processed out, still somber, the latter carrying the light of God out of the sanctuary, or at least as far as the back pew.

An hour of sitting still in a wooden pew yielded to an hour of sitting still on wooden Sunday school chairs, where the order of worship was emphasized by the order of Bible knowledge: books of the Bible, major characters of the Bible, and moralistic lessons about the meaning of Bible stories for faith in childhood. What did Paul teach? *Love does not demand its own way and must share its toys.* What did Jesus do for us? *Die on the cross so that we could feel perennially guilty for anything imperfect or errant.* What happened in the Garden of Eden? *Very bad nakedness.* Who was the best king? *David, the rebel harpist, the rapist of Bathsheba, the keeper of an international harem, the lover of Jonathan, the inspiration of assassinations, but always the best because he killed Goliath with a stone.* Ah, the things we don't tell children in Sunday school.

I loved knowing the right answers in Sunday school and watching the perfect order of our German Reformed liturgy in worship. I had less affection for the silence and stillness that appeared to be a prerequisite for all things well-ordered. I may have inherited the spirit of German stoicism, but I was still a stubborn and restless kid. Sitting politely had its limits. Distractions were inevitable. More than once during worship, after I finished coloring the children's bulletin, I would begin coloring my sisters' arms. Girls with moles and freckles on their skin, like my two sisters and me, make fabulous canvases for connect-the-dots. We borrowed my father's pens and took turns drawing on each other. At least for a few hilarious (but still quiet) minutes during the sermon, we would connect the dots to create funny faces, obscure animal outlines, and more. My left arm has a series of moles, for example, that are perfectly aligned to draw Ursa Minor, the Little Dipper. When my father caught us, the pens had to be returned. Silence that included hilarity was not appropriate to silence that should be holy. *Let all mortal flesh keep silence and not have fun.*

There was no running in the church at any time, not even on weekdays when no one else was there, and we weren't to raise our voices in that vaulted space. Like my young determination to keep order among the nursery toys, good order in the sanctuary required a certain strict adherence. It was as if the whole congregation believed fervently, even if unconsciously, in avoiding the fate of Uzzah, who died by the wrath of God for the simple sin of touching the sacred Ark of the Covenant when it wobbled uncertainly on a cart pulled by oxen.

That day in 2 Samuel was supposed to be a joyous occasion. There they all were, the crowd of ancient Israelites led by King David himself, dancing and singing and shouting—loudly, I might add, maybe even rambunctiously—with cymbals and harps and tambourines and songs. The entire parade of praise before the Ark, the holy presence of the LORD, was a grand occasion as they moved toward Jerusalem. David's reign had just been expanded to include Israel, in addition to Judah. Now God's presence could finally reside in the capital city of a unified Israel after generations of being carried through the wilderness, stolen in battles, and relocated every time the people conquered a new city. Once the Ark was in Jerusalem, there was hope that the very presence of the LORD would at last be secure among God's people.

Except that the Ark wasn't in Jerusalem yet. It was still on its way via parade, and the terrain over which the oxen plodded wasn't smooth. A shake of the cart. A moment's jostle. A precarious tilt. A quick steadying hand. And bam! The death of Uzzah by the wrath of God cooled the crowd's enthusiasm, to say the least. David was simultaneously livid and terrified. Everyone knew that the Ark of the LORD could only be approached and handled by those who had properly purified themselves to stand in God's presence, but Uzzah's errant touch was instinctive and well-intentioned. It was not as though there was time for a cleansing ritual as he made the split second decision to restrain the Ark from falling. God's outburst and lack of grace startled David, who preferred such holy violence to be focused on the battlefield and not against his own men. Too scared to continue the processional, David had the Ark temporarily stowed in the house of Obed-edom until he was certain it would guarantee him blessing rather than harm.[8]

Is that why we were constrained as children to sit quietly in the pews: because the wrath of God held such strict standards that there was no grace for noise or wiggles? Did God require children not to laugh during worship, or was that just my parents' rule? Were drawings on little girls' arms theologically anathema to God, or socially verboten to my parents? Had the well-disciplined order of worship completely cast out (or forgotten) the days of David's dancing before the LORD?

I don't mean that I wanted to dance in church. I hadn't completely lost my sense of good order and decorum. But I did want to be silly in the pew before the LORD and still have it be worshipful. I wanted to laugh when our somber order didn't quite unfold as planned, or when we all dutifully read aloud a bulletin typo ("We have singed against Thee"), or when the ceiling fans blew out the Christmas Eve candelabra, or when the tenors lost their place in the choral anthem. I wanted to worship and to be human without fearing the deadly wrath of God. I wanted to love order and still be allowed to cast a side-eye when its strict adherence seemed contrary to the very intent of worship.

With the start of college, I discovered a space where worship was both well-ordered and fully human. In a small congregation comprised of students and led by the college chaplain, we were all recruited as worship leaders and helpers, though we shared no particular experience and had a mess of ecumenical traditions among us. I could write liturgy one week and arrange altar flowers the next, not because I had any great skill but because I was invited to do so.

---

[8] 2 Samuel 6:2–12.

Students took turns setting up and serving communion. Sometimes the Welch's spilled. We always dropped crumbs around the altar. Worship was still decently ordered—praise, confession, Scripture, prayer—but we came together on Sunday mornings not to be obliged by the order but to bring life to it:

> In the name of the Creator, Redeemer and Sustainer,
> in thought, in word, and in deed,
> assured of the grace of God and full of praise.

We laughed together and kept silence together and prayed together and sang together and even danced together. The order of worship was not so sacred that it couldn't be touched for fear of God's wrath. Instead, it was the vehicle by which we understood the order of God's love. In that setting, the purpose of worship shifted for me. Fear was no longer the motivation for sitting still in my seat. Joy was all the reason I needed to sit in worship with other students.

These days, I stubbornly continue to bring my full humanity and all of my wiggles to worship. If a worship service is mine to shape and lead and preach, I play with the liturgy so that, even within its order, worshipers of all ages have room to move in mind, body, and spirit. If I am a worshiper myself, I find ways to disobediently play in the pew, to discreetly reach out and sneak an unauthorized encounter with the Holy, most frequently by #tweetingworship on Twitter:

> Almost had a liturgical panic when it looked like the acolyte might forget to take the light out of the church. #churchnerd

> If I were a cat on Blessing of the Animals Sunday, I'd be freaking out in the presence of so many dogs.

> That moment when you realize the lector who is reading scripture sounds like Ron Swanson.

Ah, blood-filled Lenten hymns—how I've missed you! Not so much.

According to the lector, the works of the flesh (which are against the Spirit) include fractions. No word on decimals.

My restless tweets in worship are probably less well-intentioned than Uzzah's fatal reaction. While he, in a split-second decision, believed that it would be disastrous to people's faith if the Ark of God fell off the cart, I'm worried that it will be a disaster if the Church doesn't realize that good order in worship needs to include grace for the fullness and imperfection of humanity. The fear of the LORD cannot guarantee perfectly executed worship, even by the most somber and spiritual worship leaders, but it just might guarantee our fear of worshiping.

A Stolen Truck Shy of a Country Song

Martha

The week after the vet said my dog had cancer, my second husband admitted to having cheated throughout our marriage. The next week, a cracked filling left me minus a tooth. Then I found fleas on my indoor cat. These things led to bills I could not pay, and I still needed to hire a divorce lawyer.

"I'm living in a very tacky soap opera," I told my best friend. I could hear a grin in her voice over the phone.

"You're a stolen truck shy of a country song."

It did feel like one of those narrative ballads. The hero, or in my case the heroine, is living life as she thinks it should be: working hard, taking good care of children and pets, volunteering at school, spending time on friendships, going to church, hitting the gym, and committing to date night. All's right with the world, at least on the surface.

> You who live in the shelter of the Most High,
>   who abide in the shadow of the Almighty,
> will say to the Lord, "My refuge and my fortress;
>   my God, in whom I trust."[1]

---

[1] Psalm 91:1–2.

In the early 2000s, as a new pastor and a new wife and a not-so-new mom, I worked out questions of faith through writing. I developed a modest reputation as a person with gifts for drawing Scripture and everyday life together. I came across as the person I was trying to be, the person I wanted to be: trusting and lovable, not anxious and striving. Then the story I had been telling myself about my second marriage gave way to the truth when my husband made his confession in a late night, cross-country video chat.

We had met through Yahoo! Personals, so perhaps bringing the relationship to an end via internet qualified as poetic justice. There had been online lies all along, not just the chats and e-mails and texts that masked the reality. As a blogger, I wrote about our happy home. My children, my husband, and even my first husband had nicknames to semi-protect their identities. I told stories about my big dogs and numerous cats, my talented offspring. I hoped to be the inverse of the bloggers who became famous for telling the painful truth about their work lives. My aim was to be funny, to keep things bright, and to keep readers coming back with winsome blog posts.

I started blogging because I felt lonely in my marriage and lonely in my professional life. I was happy to be working as the pastor of a small church, but struggling to balance church and home. While I had many wonderful colleagues who invited me to join groups for preaching preparation and ministry support, what I did not have was a friendly colleague living a life like mine: a second-time newlywed with three school-age children and all the relationship complexities pertaining thereto. My male colleagues had wives who ran interference and made sure everyone ate dinner on Saturday night and got to church on Sunday morning. My female colleagues were either of an older generation, or not as willing as I to admit that doing ministry while raising children was hard.

Getting married for a second time was not something I had ever planned on doing. When I continued in seminary after the end of my first marriage, I was the only woman in my class with three children and no spouse. I guess there has never been a country song about a divorced seminarian and her adventures, but mine would have told of late nights reading and writing papers, a long commute out of state, and a lot of questions about whether I was on the right path. I took a leave from my studies and then went back. I withdrew the next year and then returned. I dated a few guys, and even one classmate. I ran a personal ad while doing Clinical Pastoral Education one summer. Then I met the man I would marry two years later—after graduation and just before beginning my first call in a small church.

When I started blogging, I found I could write a story about my life with a calculated, droll tone. I made things sound better. My witty children were real, as were my vomiting dogs, the head lice that came home from school, and the cat that peed on the laundry. I sometimes put it all into rhyme, with the same meter as stories about the Berenstain Bears. I did not admit to myself, however, that I was crafting short fiction out of factual tales to cover the emotional absence of my husband. I could sound real without being authentic because I needed the story of a successful second marriage to be true. And, although things were never quite right, I did everything I could talk myself into being happy, satisfied, and acceptable. I had gotten it wrong the first time; I figured I couldn't afford to be wrong again.

My country song could tell the truth. It would need a twang, a sound that was wry and cynical; no lament, because I brought it all on myself.

> O Lord, deliver me,
> my life is such a mess,
> I tried to start things over,
> but I'm calling to confess.

My online audience was a Venn diagram of clergywomen, PhD candidates, adjunct professors, and moms. Long before I met any of them in person, I thought of them as my friends. The blogging circle expanded, and, while many believed the lies I told to keep myself going, a few saw through to the empty reality I did not want to reveal. Things would seem bad, and I would wonder what to do about it, and then I would write myself back to a place of peace with my cover story: She has a second marriage, and it's sexy, it's good, and it will last. I defended the second marriage not against the world, but against my own prejudices.

I grew up in a family where no one had gotten divorced, or so they said. My mother fell in love at college with a returning World War II serviceman. He had married an English girl and brought her to the U.S., but she was too homesick to stay here, and they quickly divorced. My mother's family would not accept him as a prospective husband for her. "It would kill Umma," they said, invoking the family matriarch. Never mind that Umma's father had been married three times, after his first two wives died in childbirth. Never mind that a favorite relative's divorce had been kept secret. Divorce indicated a brokenness that could not be healed in the eyes of the family elders. It did not matter whose fault it was. It simply was not done. It was a sad relief to me that my mother had already died when The Father of My Children moved out of the house.

On my father's side, also, there were no marriages that ended other than in death. Even the widowed did not remarry. A great neighborhood scandal of his youth involved a wife who left her drunken, abusive husband and returned to her childhood home with her two daughters. In my father's mind, this was the nat- ural sequence of events for a divorced woman: She should return to the shelter of her family. He never understood why I did not do the same and bring my three little children to the big house where he lived alone after my mother died. I stood my stubborn ground, explaining that I needed to finish seminary, not move farther away from it. His death six months later meant we could not have kept the home he wanted to make for us.

Jesus spoke against divorce, except in the case of adultery. Divorce met the criteria of the law of Moses, but Jesus said the law allowed for "hardness of heart" on the part of men. He described marriage as a state of being joined together. "Therefore what God has joined together, let no one separate."[2] Remarriage counted as adultery, he said. Scholars suggest Jesus knew what being cast aside would mean for a woman, particularly if she had no father or brother to take her in and protect her. Begging or prostitution would likely be her fate. Maybe Jesus wanted to see vulnerable women kept safe.

Maybe.

It seemed questionable to consider myself in that marginalized category. Although I grieved for my father, I inherited money, bought the home where I would raise my children, and continued my education. On the surface, all was well. Underneath, I felt the shame passed down from one generation to another. The church—my church—did not say no to divorced people serving in ministry, but the social rules bred into me indicated unworthiness, and they had their root in these verses from the Bible. I felt ashamed for failing, but I feared being alone. I decided to try again.

> I built a nest and feathered it
> To prove I'm doing well
> I tried to make it all look good
> But life went straight to hell.

For several years, my blogging pseudonym was Songbird. I used to sing, and I have often dreamt of flying, but the impulse to give myself that nickname comes from the early internet era. I was two years past the first divorce, hoping to meet someone again, and confused about what I wanted in life. I was lonely. I made a poor dating choice and wanted to avoid the guy on AOL Instant Messenger. I needed a new identity, not my first initial and last name. It's embarrassing to admit that I took my AOL username from Ibsen's play *A Doll's House*. Songbird is one of the nicknames the husband, Torvald, uses to assert his control over the wife, Nora. Although single, I identified

---

2 Mark 10:9.

with her. A few years later, a story from my childhood inspired this epigraph for my blog.

> Aunt Mim had a birdcage music box in her living
> room. I loved to wind it up and listen to the song-
> bird. What would she do if I set her free?

Songbird was funny and happy, busy getting children to places they were going. Songbird had friends who were eager to read her blog posts, joke around, or join a conversation in the comments. Songbird reached out to other bloggers, especially women in ordained ministry, and helped them make connections. Songbird did all these things, and there was truth in them, but there was a lie underneath it all, the fiction of a satisfying marriage that she invented—that I invented—to keep me in it. Being Songbird took up space and time that otherwise felt barren as my children needed less from me, and as I experienced the anxiety of being married to a person whose emotional distance amplified his regular geographic absences because of work.

Who kept the birdcage door closed? If I couldn't get marriage right, maybe I could get ministry right to make up for it.

> Lord, maybe if I work real hard
> You'll see I love you true
> And you'll forgive the lies I told
> to me as much as you.

One way to shield my personal life from too much attention was to keep actual people away from it. Our house, which had once been full of friends, went quiet. I used a strict understanding of pastoral boundaries to keep my church interactions at church and not bring them to my home. I worked a lot. I hope I did my job effectively, preaching and visiting and volunteering for committees and offering support to colleagues, while keeping my private situation, well, private. When a mentor asked about my marriage and I tried to explain it, he shook his head.

"It's very unusual," he said, and I thought, yes, we are special; I am doing an atypical thing and nothing is wrong with that. I convinced myself God had called me to this difficult relationship to teach me something about trust. I looked the other way so carefully that I managed to forget the things I should have seen as warning flags. I did it so well my husband said, in our fateful video chat, "I thought you knew." No.

> And when I get snared up by
> things I never should have done,
> will you help me get back out?
> I need you, Holy One.

One divorce was bad, but two? What would my family think? My kids? My colleagues, and parishioners, and the friends who thought I had a good thing going in ministry and in marriage? I could explain away one divorce, and lay the blame somewhere else, but surely people would hold me responsible this time. It was a debacle, a fiasco of my own making, indefensible.

And how would God regard me?

The decision to call the marriage done came from me, after questions asked from a distance of 2500 miles, as the clock passed midnight. In shock, I could not go to sleep; it was too late to call a friend. Lying in bed with the lights off, I held my iPhone and typed e-mails to people I hoped would love me even though my life was a disaster, people who would offer support. Maybe the one in England would wake up early. Why were my U.S. friends all in the Eastern and Central time zones? The clock moved from 1 to 2 a.m. as I sent the news out to Pennsylvania, Massachusetts, and Texas. The night had so many hours left.

I was only a few weeks into a new job. I wondered, "How will I go to the office in the morning?" "How will I keep breathing when it feels like a train hit me?" "How can I ever preach this Sunday?" In the dopiness of no sleep, my mind continued to race, as I did the math of the week. The morning would be Wednesday. I had to get myself together somehow.

I thought, "This is why people wrote psalms."

I had been reading and following the Revised Common Lectionary with close attention for twenty years, beginning in a women's Bible study when my oldest was a preschooler. The lectionary always had something to say to me. That night I turned to the texts for the coming Sunday and found Psalm 91.

> For he will deliver you from the snare
>   of the fowler
>   and from the deadly pestilence;
> he will cover you with his pinions,
>   and under his wings you will find refuge;
>   his faithfulness is a shield and buckler.[3]

If you do a Google image search for the fowler's snare, you will find a bird bound up in a cruel net. I spent a lot of years picturing myself in a birdcage. In the midst of seeking a call, I had turned down a church where the parsonage reminded me of a birdhouse on a pole. Why could I read those signs, yet not the ones I now perceived so clearly in retrospect?

> You will not fear the terror of the night,
>   or the arrow that flies by day,
>   or the pestilence that stalks in darkness,
>   or the destruction that wastes at noonday.[4]

How would God regard me? Like a bird in the snare of the fowler, like one in need of deliverance. At that moment it did not matter whether another person had set the snare, or I had set it myself. I believed God would help me get out of it.

I did not sleep that night, but I rose from my bed with a plan:

------
[3] Psalm 91:3–4.
[4] Psalm 91:5–6.

who to call, who to see, what to say, when and what to tell my children. I trembled with exhaustion, but I functioned. With the dawn, e-mails came, and then phone calls. They were all from people who knew me first as Songbird, but had, over the years, become friends with Martha. Whether they suspected the truth about my reality or not, they loved me. They showed up, mighty women filling my freezer with lasagna and rearranging the furniture and sleeping across the foot of my bed while my 130-pound dog, Sam, lay ill and restless beside me. God never wanted me to be in the birdcage or the net. God wanted to see me set myself free.

> Those who love me, I will deliver;
>   I will protect those who know my name.
> When they call to me, I will answer them;
>   I will be with them in trouble,
>   I will rescue them and honor them.
> With long life I will satisfy them,
>   and show them my salvation.[5]

In time things got better, as they should in the last verse of any worthwhile country song. I felt rueful, remorseful, and regretful for a while. I also felt repentant for lying to God and to myself. My dear dog Sam died, and so did the fleas on the cat, eventually. I saved money on the divorce by doing most of the paperwork myself. I stopped calling myself by a nickname online. I kept my sense of humor. When I got married again (yes, again) and had better dental insurance, I got an implant. I'll probably never buy a truck, though, because the last thing I need is for someone to steal it.

> Thank you, Lord, for being there,
>   all day and through the night,
>   for loving and forgiving me,
>   when I don't get it right.

---

[5] Psalm 91:14–16.

Secrets Too Deep
for Words

Rachel

The church in which I grew up had an implicit eleventh com-
mandment: Thou shalt not air dirty laundry.

I was born and raised in rural Pennsylvania, in a place where the
air is clear, except on trash-burning days and manure-spreading days.
When the weather cooperates, many households dry their washed
laundry outdoors on clotheslines. The Amish have the longest lines
for their laundry: jeans spread like upside-down Vs waving high on
a pulley system between telephone poles, button-down shirts hung
by their tails as high as the barn roof and reaching for the ground
with their long sleeves. The rest of us have clotheslines strung in our
backyards between much shorter poles, maybe only six feet tall with
lines sagging low enough that my ten-year-old self could reach up to
pin clothes during her after-school chores. Clotheslines are intended
for laundry that's been washed, of course. No one wants or expects to
see their neighbors' dirty laundry flapping in the wind. Besides, what
good is the fresh air to stained and stinky clothes?

The same principle was sacred in the social expectations at our
church. What good was saying life's problems aloud in the open, or
naming worries or messes or raw moments unabashedly, except to
embarrass those who heard it? Of the struggles that members might
consider sharing with their church family, any topic that carried even
a blush of sinfulness, by socially and theologically conservative measures, was the most taboo to air, like daring to dangle lace panties on
the clothesline instead of plain cotton ones. Concerns that were cir-
cumstantially beyond control and did not imply guilt could be shared
discretely and without detail. Thus, in worship it was acceptable to ask
for prayers related to illness or death, but there were no prayer requests

about suicide or sexuality, marital or financial problems. If they were said aloud at all, it was in private to the pastor, or the pastor's wife, or your dearest church friend.

So I learned from a young age that faith always presented a strong and composed face in public and especially at church. You wore your Sunday best, sang your Sunday hymns, learned your Sunday school lessons, got your gold star for Sunday school attendance, and went merrily on your way without telling a single soul that you were bullied in school, or that your sister or daughter was gay, or that you were ready to collapse from parenting, or that your spouse struggled with depression. (Of course, as happens in a family church, even without airing your dirty laundry, eventually the whole congregation knew.)

None of this was pretense or charade. It was a cultural interpretation of the life of faith. In sermons and in Sunday school and in the unspoken habits of church life, I learned that discipleship responded to Jesus's call with a stiff upper lip. You followed him across stormy seas and into the time of trial, even up to the place of death, and there was little room along that journey for tears or drama. You might be asked to leave behind your family, to turn away from friends, to give up everything, if Jesus so much as asked, and you shouldn't cry about it if he did. Thankfully, it seemed rare that Jesus actually asked people at church to walk away from their families, and no one I knew in the congregation felt called to give up all of their wealth and security.

Being strong and determined, unflappable and reputable: These were the demonstrations of deep faith. How did I know? Because the little paper disciples on the felt board in Sunday school never talked back to Jesus or said that it was too hard. Because the pastor never preached that life could kick your ass, or that God might actually give you more than you can handle. Because Baby Jesus was born to die for our sins, not to live with our whining. Because the purpose of Sunday school was to know all the answers, not to ask all the questions. Because no one came to church with obvious bruises on their bodies, minds, or spirits. So one day when you're grown and you find yourself yelling in the car at your husband because he has just called your son a *b*tch* for the simple sin of being a tired three-year-old, it doesn't occur to you that Jesus cares one whit about your pain because the whole point of discipleship is to carry on bravely no matter what life hands you.

Life handed me—no, let me take responsibility for my own actions—I married a mean and abusive man. He criticized the way I walked. He was alternately annoyed and irate at the way I parented. He demanded the children's playful attention when he was in a good mood and their absolute silence when he was in a foul mood. He required my willingness to cook a full meal at any hour, and when, after several years, I refused, I guaranteed myself an argument or the silent treatment. But, no matter; my faith remained a picture of strength. I went to church regularly—not only on Sundays but on weekdays too, because it was my place of employment—and, in good faith, I didn't talk about my bruises.

When Jesus and church conspire to teach you that faith has a stiff upper lip, you turn to the Holy Spirit to hold the secrets you cannot speak:

> The Spirit intercedes with sighs too deep for words.
> And God, who searches the heart, knows what is
> the mind of the Spirit.[6]

The Spirit's discretion is a miraculous ray of hope when you are holding secrets about being afraid at home, about being scared for the safety of your children, about tiptoeing through each day in order to avoid setting off your husband's anger. I held onto Romans 8:26–27 as tightly as I held myself together for those four years. *No one else has to know, but the Spirit understands what I can't articulate.*

The secrets I held could not be uttered in any form. This was no longer a matter of spiritual decorum but of sheer incapability. Sitting in a church nursery one day to talk with a local pastor while my

---

[6] Romans 8:26b–27a.

children played nearby, I sobbed and stuttered but could not form the words to express the pain in my household. Although I make sense of life through my pen, even for a writer there are words that are too awful to articulate. "Abuse" wasn't a word I allowed myself to whisper or think until almost five years after the divorce was finalized. I wouldn't, couldn't, write the word in ink or on a blog, because then it would have been visible to the whole world. The other words about my then-husband's behavior were worse. Even today I don't write them down. Bruises are not meant to be seen. And if faith isn't your concealer of choice to cover life's pains, there's a whole makeup industry known as "self-help" for your heart's hurts and your life's blemishes—memes and books and programs to make sure your bruises are masked in socially appropriate ways.

If Romans 8 was a balm to my secrecy, however, the apostle Paul's words also helped me double down on my spiritual rationale for keeping those secrets.

> The sufferings of this present time are not worth comparing with the glory about to be revealed.[7]

To paraphrase: "Congratulations, your volatile personal situation will fade in the glory of the last days." I interpreted Paul's writing as dismissive of present sufferings and of the need to name them. In the grand scheme of Christ's fulfillment, of what relevance was my husband's threat to leave our children with total strangers? If truly "all things work together for good for those who love God, who are called according to [God's] purpose,"[8] of what use was it to leave a bad marriage? Why air dirty laundry if God would make it clean in the sweet by-and-by?

Mercifully, we have some measure of control over our actual dirty laundry. Perhaps a stray sock falls out on the floor next to the washing machine and gets dirty all over again. That's okay. Maybe a bra strap strangles a sweater and you're stuck untangling the two

---

[7] Romans 8:18.
[8] Romans 8:28.

in the middle of a laundromat. Awkward, but manageable. What's
the worst that can happen with dirty clothing? It's much harder
to control the dirty laundry of life, and a significant part of mine
was aired when criminal charges were filed against my then-husband. "Pedophile" was a word that the court could say aloud, even
though I couldn't make my pen write it. And still I didn't tell my
church community. Since it was rare for church members to track
daily criminal filings at the local courthouse, no one knew except
those I brought into my confidence as a safety net.

I called out sick from my church job on the day of trial, but I
went to work the day after he skipped town. I moved out of our
apartment on a Saturday so that I could be in church on Sunday.
Routine was everything to maintain the appearance of an unfractured faith and an unfractured life.

> In all these things we are more than conquerors
> through Christ who loved us.[9]

Unable to conquer the dirty laundry of life, I was damn sure
going to conquer the performance of my faith. I spent another year
working at the church before I moved to a new state and entered
seminary fulltime, as a single mother. The move out of state and
onto a graduate school campus provided some relief from my ex's
dirty laundry and an immediate distraction for my stress. With the
Spirit holding my trauma in wordless sighs, I threw myself into the
academic achievements of faith. Writing papers for class late into the
nights meant that I was (usually) too tired for nightmares. Building
my professional skills for ministry meant solidifying my abilities to
care deeply for "the whole creation . . . groaning in labor pains,"[10]
while maintaining also the pastoral composure necessary to remain
present to the world's pain. It was a role well-suited for someone
steeped in the practice of maintaining spiritual decorum through hell
and high water. And, again, the pursuit of faith's fortitude was not

---

[9] Romans 8:37.
[10] Romans 8:22.

insincere. To be strong in the face of suffering, to be unbowed by a storm in life, was a sign of deep grounding in Christ. I had the Spirit who held onto what I could not. I trusted the Spirit to whisper it to God in good time, and, until then, I forged ahead in the confidence that Christ's glory would not be deterred just because my husband hurt and abandoned my family.

Take that, dirty laundry!

There were still times I could not control what laundry was aired and when. Having my then-husband go through a criminal trial meant it was newsworthy when he fled town after the guilty verdict. His name was in the local newspaper. His face made the morning news. I might as well have pinned a pair of grungy, holey socks to the clothesline and sent invitations for everyone to come and see. The sense of threat to my children's safety continued for years after he left, so every time we relocated, I had to talk to the schools' staff about safety protocols. Bright pink bra with sweat stains, flapping in the wind. Most recently, it was a required part of my son's college application process to specifically outline the reasons why his father's financial information was not reported with the financial aid application. I would have rather hung my most stretched-out pair of underwear on a public clothesline.

Still, if the metaphor hasn't already been carried too far, at some point we have to actually deal with our dirty laundry, and not by hanging it on the clothesline in all its filth. We can only buy new underwear for so long before we finally concede to running the washing machine. Perhaps the best result of praying desperately for the Spirit to hold my secrets was that the Spirit didn't actually keep my secrets, but whispered them into a few hearts who were willing to be God's presence to me through the crisis. Like a congregation sharing just enough whispers and hints of dirty laundry to know that a hot meal or a hospital visit was needed, a few dear people held discreet space for the words that I could not say. If, on some days, my faith and determination were completely composed and I looked confident from head-to-toe, it was fine with them. If, on other days, I had dirty laundry stuck to my pant leg because I had pulled clothes out of the hamper—literally or spiritually—that was okay with them, too.

While I continue to deepen my roots in the practice of spiritual composure, the Spirit continues to hold my quaking. While I continue to attune my spirit outward to the groanings of Creation, the Spirit continues to sing lullabies over my own inward groaning. While I continue to earnestly hold my faith together, the Spirit continues to have loose lips and whispers a holy nudging occasionally where it is needed. There are worse things in life than having the Spirit tell your secrets. I suppose I'm okay with the fact that she does.

Lost in a Labyrinth

Rachel

Is it too strong to say that I hate labyrinths? It surely is, and perhaps it is not wholly accurate. Labyrinths are artful and pleasant to study visually. I like that much about them. They're symmetrical. I find that satisfying. They are located in places that evoke a sense of hallowedness. I deeply appreciate that atmosphere. Many people I know love and study and regularly use labyrinths. I mean no offense.

Still, it is utterly true to confess that I don't understand the point of labyrinths or the spiritual discipline of walking them. I mean, I understand the concept. There's a path. It leads to the center—no detours, no optional branches, no dead-ends. Just a singular winding path that makes its way to a center and then out again without distractions. In other words, it leads nowhere. Twice. Inward, outward, inward, outward, like a playground swing going forward and backward, but a labyrinth doesn't go higher or increase with intensity, and there's no wind whooshing on your face, and there's no sweat as you pump your legs hard, and there's no heart-stopping moment when you decide to leap without knowing how you will land. It's just forward and backward, inward and outward.

I watch people walking labyrinths in their calm, meditative way, and I wonder what profundity they find in the experience, what revelation appears with each winding turn, or what peaceful illumination reveals itself at the blissful center. I walk those same labyrinth paths, and . . . nothing. No revelation. No realization. I count my steps until I get bored. I study the landscaping: Vacation-Bible-School-painted rocks, pristinely sculpted paths, tall hedges, flagstones winding through mown grass. I pretend to be deep in thought. I calculate the best pace to ensure that I don't catch up to the spiritually-focused walker in front of me. I wonder why I am walking in circles when I could very well be walking toward a destination. Halfway through the course it occurs to me that I should have entered the labyrinth with a question held lightly in my heart so that, at the center, an answer might appear like wisdom emerging on a Magic 8 Ball. I stare at my shoes and aimlessly chew a fingernail when I reach the center. Truly profound.

Of course, I understand the parallel between the destination-less journey of a labyrinth and the wandering journeys of life and faith. Our destinations and goals change often across our lifetimes. Our faith shifts and twists, turns and grows. We wander with intention—or not. We can't ever be anywhere along the path except where we are. Faith is best lived when we practice being present along the journey to God, to ourselves, to one another. I get it. Nevertheless, traveling without a purpose frustrates me, and I don't understand any logic that suggests you should take the longest route possible between two points. The most efficient way for a labyrinth traveler to find themselves in the desired center is simply to walk straight across all of the rings. Why doesn't anyone do that? Why don't more people skip over the borders and make a beeline for the center?

For hundreds of years, the spiritual practice of meditating along the path of a circle has been etched into the sacred spaces of cathedrals and church camps, fields and gardens, stones and pottery. For hundreds of years, Christians have adopted the labyrinth as a symbol of pilgrimage. For hundreds of years, Christians have found meaning in the labyrinth's opportunity for reflection. For hundreds of years, Christians have called it an exercise in faith to walk in circles. Maybe Christians haven't noticed that the Church doesn't need a map on the floor to spend its time walking in circles. But I digress.

It's a long-revered (if by "revered" we mean "aggravating") experience of faith to travel without going anywhere. The ancient Israelites, on the verge of tasting the milk and honey of the Promised Land, were turned back by God and compelled to wander for an additional forty years. That was their faith assignment: Just wander, stare at the rocks, scrounge for food, watch the babies grow into toddlers and the youth into adults who themselves would birth a new generation before being allowed to cross into the Promised Land. Similarly, Jesus spent his entire ministry walking from place to place, not settling down, calling people to leave their homes just for the joy of wandering with him. He visited towns and temples, strangers and friends. Whether people wanted him to stay or leave, he kept going. If the mountaintop view was glorious, he walked on. If a crowd's need for healing was extensive, he did what he could without delaying his journey. Occasionally he added variety by traveling in a boat or walking across water or riding on a donkey. I wear different shoes for the same reason—not because the path is any different, but because a little variety on my feet is nice along the way.

My father used to say, "This road will take you anywhere," when I thought we were lost on a back country road. (To his credit, I don't think my father ever really gets lost.) Like the labyrinth, Dad's reassurance conveyed joy in the journey and trust that the destination would be there whenever we arrived. Unlike the labyrinth, however, our family excursions actually ended up somewhere; there was a real destination at the end of our wandering, some place that held far more appeal than the center of a rippling pattern of loops. It could be a roller skating rink or a riverside restaurant, the local hoagie shop or summer church camp. My memory immediately ranks those destinations. The riverside restaurant offered the bonus activity of skipping rocks after dinner, so long as you were careful to avoid goose droppings. Roller skating was a risk-your-bones kind of thrill, especially if I tried to stay in the rink after the announcer called, "Backwards skate only." Church camp was formative and fabulous: rock climbing and creek hiking and flashlight tag and knowing the right answers in Bible studies, but it was also the longest of our regular road trips. As a kid who quickly felt queasy in the back seat, I didn't have much fondness for taking the back roads to camp. The hoagie shop easily wins as the best destination after a car ride, especially the long-gone

Cozy Corners restaurant where our family played pool after eating dinner.

That's the crux of it, for me: having the destination. Labyrinths lack a place to go, an end goal, and therefore to me they lack a purpose. What type of person is content to weave along the wandering labyrinth path, knowing they will only return to the same place? What peace do they find along the way? What mindfulness do they practice while walking? Do some people try to keep their hearts and minds clear in a labyrinth? Is the space freeing, or is the appeal in its controlled pattern? Is there a spiritual pot of gold at the end of the labyrinth that I'm just not seeing?

More often than I intend, I find myself in the shoes of Zacchaeus, whose fear of missing out (FOMO) on the hype about Jesus compelled him to climb a sycamore tree. Why were so many people crowding to see this teacher and healer? What was Zacchaeus missing while busily managing his tax collector duties? Clearly, he took his work seriously and did it well enough to be designated as *chief* tax collector. A disciplined professional like Zacchaeus probably kept his curiosities under control. There were books to attend to, money to measure, treasuries to dutifully fill. A man with those responsibilities would have been careful not to venture too far outside the lines of regulations and routines, less he be found unreliable or untrustworthy.

The whispering about Jesus must have caused significant curiosity that Zacchaeus was driven to satisfy by weaving his way through the crowds in an effort to see this teacher who had come to Jericho. He climbed a tree like a schoolboy—how terribly unlike the dignified rich man that he was. Zacchaeus was so caught up in his spiritual FOMO that he found himself peering down at Jesus from the branches. Just as he was wondering how an ordinary and dusty man could cause such a ruckus in the city, Jesus stopped and looked up at him.

"Zacchaeus, hurry and come down; for I must stay at your house today."[1]

The fear of missing out can cause us to do funny things.

---

[1] Luke 19:5.

Zacchaeus scrambled down the tree, getting his hands dirty and catching his robes on the sycamore's tattered bark, just for the chance to go from *missing out* to *being in the middle of it*. They had lunch, and Zacchaeus had a conversion moment: He would make reparations for his cheating scams, redistribute his wealth to the poor, and set his heart on faithful living. By the time lunch ended, the heavens opened and the angels sang.

Maybe people are experiencing angels while they walk labyrinths—helper angels, messenger angels, an angelic choir, invisible guides who whisper holy thoughts along the way. Maybe that's why I don't *see* anything as I watch people walk.

Of course, not every case of spiritual FOMO turns out well. Peter met with a terrifying and very wet end as a result of FOMO. Sleepy from pulling the night watch with the other disciples as their boat crossed the sea, he was startled by the vision of a ghost walking on the water toward the boat. The early morning light made the haze shift and play in the disciples' imaginations, and they all shouted in fright. When Jesus called out in reassurance, Peter was consumed by the desire to do exactly what Jesus was doing. He wanted to walk on water. FOMO plus fatigue—a dubious combination. "Come," Jesus said,[2] and Peter leapt out of the boat and took a few successful steps before realizing—as most of us would—"Holy shit, I have no actual experience walking on water." With the strong wind around him, deep water beneath him, and Jesus still only an apparition in front of him, Peter began to sink in fear.

It's amazing, the lengths to which we will go to glean from one another's faith practices instead of finding our own, or the time we will invest in jealous examination and imitation of one another's spiritual habits. I have tried to walk labyrinth after labyrinth to cull meaning from the experience. Clearly the winding walk is meaningful to others. What is wrong with me that I find the exercise pointless? I try again, and enter a circular path lined with stones brightly painted by summer campers. What am I missing from my

---

2 Matthew 14:29.

view in the sycamore tree that everyone else can see? I try again, this time on a rolled-out fabric labyrinth inside a church, where candles and soft music set a somber tone. What faith skill am I missing to walk on water or wander a labyrinth successfully?

What shapes a person's affinity for certain spiritual practices more than others?

After many attempts, my FOMO faded. I became willing to accept that labyrinths aren't my cup of tea. I was never one who liked getting dizzy anyway. Instead I have found a large cemetery that stretches across several steep hills, with plenty of shade from the enormous rock oak trees, and thousands of headstones ranging from elegant to creepy to heartbreaking. There are no walking paths here, only a few winding roads for cars. I like walking without a path and meandering wherever a distraction prompts me to go. An eroded angel prompts me to walk uphill. A Celtic cross inspires me to stroll downhill. I scuff through the grass and peak at the mausoleums. If I dare to stare through their windows, I can see the stained glass and altars inside. Death being the great equalizer, there are headstones for babies and matriarchs, priests and soldiers. I love to read what people say about their faith on their tombstones, what words of love and remembrance are written to those who have passed away.

Other people wander through the cemetery, too, usually at a distance, but I don't wonder why they're here, or what they're thinking, or how their faith is doing, or whether I will inadvertently catch up with them as I walk. I suppose my roaming in the cemetery lacks a destination even more than the labyrinth. Then again, cemeteries put "destination" into serious perspective. Wandering through the cemetery relieves my labyrinth FOMO. There's no need to follow a prescriptive course. There's no need to reach a certain center or to have a particular epiphany. There's no need for my feet and my spirit to worry about where they're going when I'm in a cemetery. There is only the need to be.

The Nine of Swords

Martha

My stomach roiled as I climbed the stairs to her office. Everything I touched—the railing, the door knob—felt prickly, as if some sort of dark static electricity coursed through it. The woman who greeted me seemed calm and sensitive, but my unrest continued to bubble. Introductions made, we sat across from each other on floor cushions, and she opened the silky cloth wrapped carefully around a deck of cards. She spread it out on the floor between us, and then shuffled the cards once, twice, three times.

The cards, larger than the deck I used for solitaire, made a soft sound as they mixed. Returning the deck to the cloth she asked me to cut the cards twice. She re-stacked them and invited me to make as many small piles as I wanted. When I finished, she looked at them for a moment, and then picked them up in what seemed like no particular order, perhaps following some instinct.

"Cut them again," she said, and after I complied, "Once more." She held the deck up; it seemed like she listened to it. Satisfied, she went to work and laid out the cards—ten of them—face down, in a spread called the Celtic Cross. The cards, their names, and the images carry archetypal meanings, and a tarot reader interprets them based on their individual positions in the spread as well as the overall arrangement of cards. Your situation or question, what "crosses" you, what lies beneath the surface, what is behind you, what is coming in the near future, your hopes and fears, all make an appearance in the reading.

As the cards turned over, I tried to take in the symbolism, but they were new to me, and it all felt overwhelming. The only card I remember from that reading is the one that sat to the left of all the others, representing the near past. Pictured on the Nine of Swords was an ambiguous figure, sitting up in bed, head in hands. The bed was carved, the garment could have been a nightdress of any era, and the quilt across the knees was a patchwork of flowers interspersed with astrological signs. Behind the seated figure, nine swords stretched out, above and parallel to the bed, on a black background. That weeping woman is me, I thought, awake in the night, troubled by nightmares and terrible thoughts. That weeping woman is me.

> O LORD, do not rebuke me in your anger,
>   or discipline me in your wrath.
> Be gracious to me, O LORD, for I am
>   languishing;
>   O LORD, heal me, for my bones are shaking
>   with terror.
> My soul also is struck with terror,
>   while you, O LORD—how long?[3]

It was the summer that my first husband moved out of the house. Our children were ten, five, and not quite one. I had twenty-one seminary credits out of the ninety needed for my Master of Divinity, and I could not see how I was going to finish school. Suffering from a lengthy and severe postpartum depression, I spent that summer grasping at all kinds of straws. My father, rightly worried about me, encouraged me to get out of the house and do something. I signed up for a tarot class. Twenty years later, I don't remember why it seemed like a good idea. After I registered, I scheduled a private reading. In that season of disorientation, a trial run seemed like the only way to ensure I wouldn't get lost on the way to class.

The woman sitting across from me came to work with the tarot from a background of art history and counseling. I knew her name because she had done a program for the local C.G. Jung Center where my mother-in-law worked. While my mother-in-law and I shared interests like knitting and Jane Austen, she also introduced me to things on the banned list in my household growing up: psychology, astrology,

---

[3] Psalm 6:1–3.

numerology, and tarot. If you visit a fortune teller, you might find a dog-eared deck on the table, but I assumed anything approved by the Jung Center had to be more meaningful, less superstitious. Yet what I really wanted was a fortune teller. I wanted someone to tell me that around the corner I would find love and happiness, that I would not end up on the discard pile or be left in the remainder of the deck of cards, unplayed and unread.

I still felt the tingle as I left the tarot reader that night, and I looked around as I returned to my car. From somewhere in the great beyond, my Baptist grandmother had to be aiming a lightning bolt. She held a hostility toward all practices that could be considered vaguely magical. My brother and I were not allowed to have a Ouija board, that popular staple of slumber parties originally devised as a parlor game. In her mind, it represented one of many things that got in the way of being a faithful Christian. Since she had been a missionary, she held some family authority on those matters. Rock musicals about Jesus, Magic 8 Balls, and newspaper horoscopes all qualified as anathema.

As I drove home, I pushed back the rising shame and methodically reconstructed the shape of the reading and the images on the cards.

> Turn, O LORD, save my life;
>> deliver me for the sake of your steadfast love.
> For in death there is no remembrance of you;
>> in Sheol who can give you praise?[4]

Your situation, that's what the first card represents—your situation or your issue. I was thirty-five, trying to figure out how to stay alive and find a new identity as I came to realize that my separation was going to become a divorce. Whether the marital breakdown caused the depression or the other way around, my issue, my situation, had become life threatening. Six days in the psychiatric unit of the local

---

[4] Psalm 6:4–5.

hospital, a diagnosis of major depression, and a prescription for Zoloft only exacerbated the marital difficulties.

The second card is laid over it crosswise; it is actually called the crossing card. My dad wanted to help me. A lawyer himself, he hired the most aggressive lawyer he could find. Of course my father wanted to protect me, but his fury at my husband hurt as much as it helped. I needed financial support from both of them, and I didn't have the wherewithal to tell them they were making life harder for me.

The third card is positioned below the first two, a card representing what lies beneath. I was still depressed. I was taking antidepressants that kept me awake, and another medication that made me sleep so deeply I could not stop myself from chewing on the inside of my mouth. Instead of asking for help, I stopped taking my meds. When I finally told the psychiatrist, she said, "That wasn't very kind to your brain."

I do not remember the cards that sat in the first three positions. I only remember the next one, that Nine of Swords. Jeanne, the reader, paused. I remember how kind her face was, and the compassion in her eyes. Before that day, I thought of myself as someone who didn't "get" symbolism. I never took Art History. Although I liked art museums, I mostly loved portraits or paintings of recognizable Bible stories or myths. When I was a little girl, my father would take me to the National Gallery of Art. I had a preference for Renoir's various little girls, with their watering cans and hoops. I saw myself in them, imagined myself in their lovely clothes, wished for their long hair, and invented lives for them off the canvas.

Now on a three-by-five card, not much bigger than the ones I used to play solitaire or bridge or Crazy Eights, I saw myself in the ambiguous figure, head in hands, bent in sorrow. Those swords! They reminded me of dark thoughts in the night, of dreams ending in disaster despite a doped-up sleep.

"This card seems to mean something to you," said Jeanne.

"I am that woman. That woman in the bed is me." The woman seemed so much like me to me that it is only now, more than twenty years later, that I see the figure has no gender. Anxiety and suffering are universal.

> I am weary with my moaning;
> every night I flood my bed with tears;
> I drench my couch with my weeping.[5]

In Psalm 6, the writer describes a grief process that sounds like a deep depression. The person speaking wonders if God is angry: How much longer will this suffering continue? They ask for deliverance in this life. Their weeping lasts through the night, exhausting the spirit and the body, telling us that deep hopelessness and grief are not modern inventions. People have experienced loss forever, and some have felt like nothing good would ever come again. And they cried out to God, even in the midst of misery.

The suit of Swords in the tarot deck is associated with the element of air, and with thinking and the mind. The Nine in each of the suits indicates a not-quite-complete condition. Each resolves with number Ten. The classic interpretation of the Nine of Swords indicates mental anguish, nightmares, a fear of looking at what's actually around, suggested by the hands covering the face. I wish I could say the next card is more cheerful, but it shows a figure stabbed by ten swords. The only note of hope is a rising sun in the distance. But it is a note of hope.

The reading continued, and we moved into cards that pointed to possibilities and the future, which was what I really wanted to hear. That was what I came for: some sign of life, some glimpse of anything new on the horizon, some potential happy ending.

Separation from my husband led to separating from the identity of wife and the role of spouse. It also meant redefining my relationships with friends. I had never noticed that I didn't talk to my friends over the weekend. Suddenly I was alone on Friday night and all day Saturday while my kids were with their dad. I wanted to talk to someone, but did not feel I had the right to interrupt my friends'

---

[5] Psalm 6:6.

family time. I knew from our weekday conversations in the day camp pickup line or on the playground that they and their husbands were shocked by the separation. "How could he leave his children?" a neighbor dad asked his wife. I wondered why she repeated it to me. Sometimes our attempts to show support only show how uncertain the ground is after the personal earthquake.

Many of my women friends were from church, and they overlapped with women I knew through my sons' preschool and a babysitting co-op. When I came out of the hospital, they provided meals for several weeks. My Bible study sisters chipped in to pay a cleaning lady to come and get my house in order, and one of them came over to help pick things up before the cleaner arrived. You know a person is showing Christian love when she will pick up the Legos strewn all over your house. They understood depression, or at least they understood that I was in trouble. But the separation felt intolerable. Our marital failure had highlighted the weak points in the girders of their relationships, the cracks in the foundations of their marriages. All marriages have imperfections. Some couples develop better relationship skills, or hold on more determinedly, or face more family pressure to stay together. My situation exposed the vulnerability they felt; many of them were moms who stayed home full time with kids, wives who did not know what they would do without the breadwinner keeping things together.

> My eyes waste away because of grief;
> they grow weak because of all my foes.[6]

I felt the loss of their companionship, of the understanding we share with people living a life like ours at an unconscious level that we don't have to discuss. And because I was already depressed, this change in those relationships devastated me. Almost everyone began to feel like some kind of a foe. People living ordinary lives had something I did not have anymore. Good relationships began to seem like a scarce resource.

---

[6] Psalm 6:7.

It took a decade for me to look back and see how long depression lingered: three years, maybe four. Even under that cloud, I had to make decisions. We moved twice in just over a year, from the house sold in the divorce, to a rental, and then into another house after my father died and left me in a position to own a home again. My realtor was a guy from church, the place that supplied almost all of my connections. We had been looking for a few weeks when he called and asked if I could come and see a house right away. The house was bargain priced, on a very nice dead-end street in an established neighborhood in Portland, and within walking distance of an elementary school and a middle school. He expected a bidding war, and told me we only had an hour's window to see it.

It was February. Snow capped the overgrown hydrangeas in the front yard. Everything in the house was so dirty that I pulled myself in as small as I could get, avoiding door jambs and knobs. Packing boxes stacked against a wall obscured the size of one bedroom; nicotine filmed the ceiling of another; and the carpet in the living room bore the unmistakable stains and odors of dogs not let outside in time. The French doors and sunroom windows might be charming once the filthy sheers came down, but there were so many broken panes. I hurt for that house, clouded by its own gloom, grim in its distress.

That sad house and I connected. My bid won. Sixty days later, the house was empty but still filthy, and I walked through it with a general contractor and got a quote for all the work that needed to be done. After he left, the carpenter I planned to use, who happened to be my ex-husband's brother, Steven, said, "I think you could do that yourself. I'll be here every day and help keep an eye on things."

I wasn't sure I could do anything. I was so depressed, a year past hospitalization, that I spent most of the time the kids were at school lying on the couch doing absolutely nothing. I hurt all over, just like the house. But Steven seemed sure I could do it, so every weekday morning for the next six weeks, I got the kids off to their schools and I went to say hello to that sad, dirty house. I wandered through the rooms, picked out paint colors, and arranged furniture in my mind.

I met with the glazier, and the painters, and the electrician, and the guy who sanded the floors. I washed walls. I worked on the kitchen myself. The floor was a mess. The huge tiles were worn down, and some were missing. They adhered so poorly that I was able to pull most of them up myself by hand. I used a crowbar for the worst of them. That house needed me and I needed the house. I needed it to remember I could do something besides feel sad.

> Depart from me, all you workers of evil,
>   for the LORD has heard the sound of
>   my weeping.
> The LORD has heard my supplication;
>   the LORD accepts my prayer.
> All my enemies shall be ashamed and
>   struck with terror;
>   they shall turn back, and in a moment
>   be put to shame.[7]

The Psalms were written not for personal lament and celebration, but for the use of people who were suffering or rejoicing and didn't have the gift of finding the images that helped work things through for them. At the end of a lament, there is a word of praise for God: thanksgiving that the hard times are over, and the enemies—whether actual or in our brain chemistry—cannot overcome us.

When I bought my own deck of tarot cards, there were cards I hoped to see and others I dreaded. The deck includes Death and the Devil, but they don't represent what their titles say. The deck includes The Lovers, but their meaning isn't obvious either. There was nothing magical about them, of course, but really nothing fearful either. Family lore suggested that my grandmother's bias against the occult came from her years just after she was widowed in her fifties. Frantic to feel some connection to her departed husband, she went to psychics and spiritualists. I can only guess that they disappointed her.

---

[7] Psalm 6:8–10.

Or maybe she just got better.

The last four cards in a Celtic Cross sit to the right, ascending, Seven, Eight, Nine, Ten: yourself, your environment, your hopes and fears, and, finally, your outcome. I remember every single time either Jeanne or I laid them out, I hoped something good would come from each one—some symbol of hope, of life, of love. I remember how she watched my face, and the way she would turn over another card or two, or check the card at the bottom of the deck. She never pretended to predict anything. Instead she helped me keep turning things over until I could do it myself.

That woman in the bed was me. That woman flipping floor tiles was me. That woman getting better was me.

Three Cups of Coffee

Martha

Before a Starbucks on every corner was a thing, long before anyone dreamed of putting them in grocery stores, and in the days when I thought the ability to order a fancy cup of half-caf-no-foam latte was only a late-nineties joke about Niles on *Frasier*, I accepted an invitation to meet a new friend for coffee.

We had known each other for years, but in very specific roles. Lisa ran a non-profit children's theater; I brought my kids to auditions, rehearsals, and performances. We waved; we smiled; we rarely talked. Then our lives shifted. I became the divorced seminarian. She became the graduate student, entering an MA program at the seminary near Boston where I was pursuing my MDiv. When we ran into each other on campus, she surprised me by suggesting we get together back home in Portland. She seemed like one of the cool kids to me. I felt flattered to be asked. Excited.

On the appointed Friday afternoon in the late fall, I drove to Portland's Old Port a little early to seek out a parking spot. I made certain I had change for the meter and knew where to find the Starbucks. Over-preparing as a workaround for anxiety is a useful life skill. Once inside, I listened carefully to the orders of people in line ahead of me, managed to request a cup of coffee without sounding inept, and then sat down to have coffee with Lisa.

I don't remember what I wore, which is strange for me. So often my first memory of an important event is how I looked and what kind of impression I might have made. I remember a gray afternoon outside and people on the sidewalk in that popular shopping area passing the large windows, blurring as they moved away from us like the background of an important scene in a movie. The light told the audience where to focus: on the two women intent upon their conversation, one in a white shirt that illuminated her as the center of interest.

We talked about what we were studying, how she might use a masters in theology and the arts, and whether or not I would go on to be a pastor or switch to a degree program in psychology and religion instead. Although it had been a long time since I had acted in high school, I easily fell into that funny role I sometimes adopted with men in which I knew more than they thought I did about their area of expertise. It seemed to increase my pleasure in listening to her. My coffee got cold, but I sat with my hand around the cup, glamoured by her talk and by her talking. When I finally got up to go to the bathroom, I noticed how dark it was and checked the time. We had been talking for almost four hours.

"I guess I ought to go," I said when I returned to the table, but I did not want to leave. I wanted to stay with her.

"When can we get together again?" she asked, pulling out her date book.

We met often after that, always setting up the next meal or coffee before we parted. She loaned me books about theater. When she got comp tickets to a performance by a touring opera company, she invited me to go with her. We planned a nice dinner out before the opera, because isn't that what people do? I remember standing in the bathroom at my house, putting on makeup, which I did not do often.

"This feels like getting ready for a date." I spoke the words only to myself, but I could not take them back. Sometimes we get a glimmer of what we really want, of something we actually desire. Sometimes it's not the thing other people have told us we should want.

One spring afternoon, we met in the modern dance studio where my boys took classes, a big, uneven room in a building full of artists.

In the natural light of the large windows, I saw all the things I liked best about her, the things I found most attractive. In the wall-length dancers' mirror I saw myself for the first time. I felt like myself for the first time. I had to carry that thought home and consider it. It kept me up, it pressed on me. I rested uneasily with myself, agitated by feelings for someone I had never touched. I began to talk me out of myself. I convinced myself that everyone was a little bit in love with Lisa. I convinced myself that what I thought of as her boyishness meant I really must like men after all. What would a woman see in me, anyway? I romanced myself in her name and then broke up with me, because I was afraid.

> I am the LORD your God, who brought you out of the land of Egypt, out of the house of slavery; you shall have no other gods before me.[1]

When the Israelites left Egypt to go home to a place they did not know, they had some sense of their religious heritage, but they did not have a rulebook to suit their time and place. Their practices were suspect to Pharaoh, and generations of living in the middle of polytheistic culture had, no doubt, subjected them to influences that further confused each succeeding generation. By the time they realized they were wandering in the wilderness, their first impulse was to make an idol of the kind they had seen their Egyptian neighbors and masters worship. God put Moses in charge, but Moses didn't know any more than the rest of them. He had been raised in the Egyptian court and had run away to save his own life. The last thing he had wanted was to go back and talk to Pharaoh, to lead that crew of slaves and servants to some obscure freedom. After God spoke as directly to him as God has spoken to anyone, being a shepherd—safe, isolated—was no longer a choice he could make. He needed help to manage the human flock, and to do so he needed those ten commandments carved on tablets, spelling out the expectations. God

---

[1] Deuteronomy 5:6–7.

brought them out of the past, out of slavery and servitude, out of a place where they had to play by another culture's rules. God commanded, "Don't put anyone or anything before me."

My mother dressed her children in red, white, and blue because there would always be a pair of socks or a sweater to go with any outfit she chose. These were simplifications that created order and prevented missteps. There were right ways and wrong ways. She kept us safe in a fenced-in backyard and protected herself with a hedge of respectability. So when I felt myself becoming . . . myself . . . in fear I hesitated, and I thought of her, and I returned to the gods I knew: the polite household gods of Southern Christian virtue who said that women determined their success in life by the marriages they made. The power of a woman lay in being someone a man would want to marry, in maintaining his loyalty (if not his interest). For a girl who never quite fit in, it seemed like an easy rule to follow, as simple as color coordination. I might have gotten it wrong the first time, failed at being lovable enough to keep him around, but maybe I could get it right if I tried again. According to those household gods, a man could make it right.

It never occurred to me that real power meant having agency, meant knowing what and who I wanted.

A dozen years after Lisa invited me for coffee—we can mark the era by how readily I could order a tall-nonfat-no-whip mocha without irony—I asked my friend, Karla, to meet me at a different Starbucks, this one in Portsmouth, New Hampshire, halfway between my home in Maine and the Boston suburb where she lived with her wife and served a United Church of Christ congregation. I reached out to her because I needed to talk to someone who would understand. Although ours was a newish friendship and I only knew a little of her story, I trusted her.

It was summer. Outside the picture windows, the sun shone on the brick sidewalks of another tourist destination. It wasn't the first time we had met for coffee, but it was the first time I would tell someone, tell anyone, who I thought I was. My internal monologue went something like: "Breathe. Breathe, Martha. She won't be mean to you. For Pete's sake, she has a wife. But I am fifty. Won't it seem ridiculous? Won't I? I mean, who takes this long to figure things out? And what an idiot I must seem: I've had TWO husbands!" I prayerfully considered making up something else to talk about.

"So, what's going on, friend?"

I had never trusted anyone with what I was about to say, but I had made the appointment as much with myself as with her. I took a deep breath. And another. She waited. Thank God for her patience.

"It seems so silly," I said, "at my age, but I think maybe I'm not straight. And I think maybe . . . I'm in love with a woman."

"Have you ever thought this might be true before?"

It was good to have such a gentle person to talk to, one who knew the way to ask the right questions. I had done such a good job of convincing myself I could not be gay when I was in my mid-thirties that everything important about that time was more myth than memory. I remembered coffee with Lisa, but even before that, I remembered a day earlier that same year when I had my television tuned to the Boston Pops while fixing dinner. I glanced at the screen to figure out whose voice it was I found so appealing. I felt a sort of *thunk* deep inside, and a sensation of warmth that I did not know yet to call desire. "He's handsome," I thought.

"He" was the lesbian singer, k.d. lang.

That story poured out, and more like it—moments of recognition and desire I had pushed away: the butch in the convenience store, a woman from church, a neighbor, each of whom had stirred me in the late nineties, the time when I thought a lot about who and what I really found desirable until I decided it was too dangerous. I told myself we were all on a spectrum, and what I liked about women was when they were like guys; so I must really like men.

In the dozen years between the cups of coffee I drank with Lisa and Karla, I had put all those moments in a box and shoved the box to the back of the closet. I literally hid the journals I had kept and password-protected the documents on my computer. When I thought of that time, I made it a joke, which I repeated to Karla: In my thirties, I went through a Lesbian Wannabe Phase.

She smiled. "Well, don't you think it's okay to be gay?"

In my ministry, I had become an ally for LGBT inclusion in local churches and the Church at large. My kids grew up in a household where the possibility of being gay was considered matter-of-factly. As a person and a pastor, I advocated for anti-discrimination laws and marriage equality.

"I guess I think it's okay for other people, but somehow it didn't feel okay for me." Awkward. That was awkward. Karla was a good friend to hear my words with grace. She knew, more than I, how complicated it was to come out, to process assumptions planted in our minds, often by the Church, before we knew how to think it all through for ourselves.

It is true that in the 1990s, when the thoughts first crossed my mind and stirred up my insides, I wondered if it wouldn't be one more question mark that threatened my ordination process: "Depressed? Divorced? What, gay, too? How did she not know that?" I confessed to Karla that I had convinced myself years ago that it would be less complicated to deny the desires I began to identify. They were the first desires I ever had that were mine. No rulebook recommended them. No mother approved them. No one else told me I should have them.

We began to unpack the things I feared. Our denomination affirmed the value of LGBTQ+ people. I didn't have to be afraid for my job. The denomination of the woman I now loved, however, still had some work to do. Would being with me jeopardize her livelihood? Would she be willing to do that? For me? Could I risk my newly-opened heart? Over coffee with Karla, I admitted what an idol I had made of acceptance—by my family, by the Church, by some imagined judge of my feminine success.

> You shall not make for yourself an idol, whether
> in the form of anything that is in heaven above, or
> that is on the earth beneath, or that is in the water
> under the earth. You shall not bow down to them

or worship them; for I the LORD your God am a
jealous God, punishing children for the iniquity
of parents, to the third and fourth generation of
those who reject me, but showing steadfast love to
the thousandth generation of those who love me
and keep my commandments.[2]

Iniquity is a five-dollar word for sin. It carries a nuance of purposeful wrongdoing for me, whether or not that is the dictionary
definition. What parent would want to be guilty of iniquity, passing
on difficulty for generations to come? I wanted to be a parent who
encouraged her children to be themselves, and to know what they
loved to do, and to pursue those loves. It certainly sounded hypocrit-
ical and sinful, even iniquitous, to open the world to possibility for
my children but close it for myself. I have often preached that we find
our salvation in being who God made us to be, yet I had spent half
a life trying to be someone else, making a false idol of being straight.
Should I respond to the yearning I could not deny and the love that
pointed to a truth I had been afraid to live? If I believed God made
me in a particular way, if I believed what I taught my children and
preached to anyone who had listened, the answer was yes.

I measured our hours of conversation consciously, gratefully.

When we parted on the sidewalk, Karla said, "I'm happy for you,
friend."

There's a big difference between being excited for someone to love
you and being excited about loving another person. As I had tried to
understand it all by myself, I had not seen that my orientation went
beyond the physical desire. Now my heart felt drawn to one particular woman, to Kathryn, and instead of noticing the attraction
and talking myself out of it, I let myself feel it long enough to recognize that body, mind, and spirit all lit up at the sight of her. When
she brushed my foot with hers, it felt like lightning. I came out of

---

[2] Deuteronomy 5:8–10.

my closet enough to say, "You just did that so you could touch me." Then I reassured her, "I don't feel the same about seeing you that I do about our other friends. I feel excited. I feel stupidly excited." She felt the same. Thank God.

Our hearts pulled together with irresistible force, and (not but) we took our time to listen for God, to live through a long season of prayer and discernment, to keep talking to people we trusted, to hear whether this was as good as we thought it might be—good for us and for those we loved. Our kids loved us, saw our love for each other, and came to love us together. In that same season of love, the nation started to catch up with us, first one state at a time, then all of them together.

> I am the LORD your God, who brought you out of
> the land of Egypt, out of the house of slavery; you
> shall have no other gods before me.[3]

God brought me out of my past, out of servitude to our heteronormative culture's rules. I discovered that what I believed for other people I needed to apply to me, too. If I did not, I was rejecting God's steadfast love. We are not saved by conforming to what the world expects from us. God saves us by bringing us to ourselves.

Today I write and dream looking out the window at my prayer tree and, beyond it, the steeple of the Presbyterian church where my wife is the pastor. Every morning, I hear the beautiful sound of Starbucks beans being ground in our coffee maker. Every morning, I have coffee with Kathryn.

---

[3] Deuteronomy 5:6–7.

My Chai Runneth Over

Rachel

I first brought my grief to Starbucks in 2003 in order to tell a friend that my marriage was ending and that my then-husband was the defendant in a criminal trial. Many people seek out a religious space for such a sensitive conversation, perhaps the office of their priest or rabbi, but being employed by the Church compromises the ability of sacred spaces to also be sanctuary spaces for me, as I've written elsewhere.[4] So a Starbucks table it was for my confession of sadness and fear and anger. Under a dim café sconce my grieving heart found solace in a friend's presence and a grande cup of chai latte.[5] My trembling breath found a reason to slow down, inhaling the aroma of spices, exhaling to cool the hot drink. My soul's ache found a busy and blissfully anonymous space where its story wasn't the all-consuming center of the universe. My tense and weary body found a caffeinated timer: sixteen ounces by which to measure a few moments' stillness.

Grande chais quickly became ventis, and a one-time solace became a daily habit. The warm smoothness of a green mermaid cup between my hands, the bite of spices on my tongue and throat, the easy smiles of baristas who knew my name and my preferred concoction all became touchstones of comfort and normalcy in my upended world. They steeled me against the sorrow and stress that threatened to overwhelm each day. They cemented what I believed to be a necessary mask of "I'm fine" at work and home.

Every time I have moved—an average of once every three years

---

[4] Rachel G. Hackenberg, "Soccer and Starbucks," in *There's a Woman in the Pulpit* (Woodstock, VT: Skylight Paths, 2015).

[5] In the world of Starbucks, *grande* is medium, *venti* is large, *tall* is (ironically) small, and *trenta* is the holy grail.

since that first chai in 2003—Starbucks baristas have known my
name before my neighbors did. Every time I travel, whether on business trips or to soccer games, I track down the caffeinated siren.
When I need a good cry, I detour for another cup. When I feel on
top of the world, I stride in to celebrate myself. When the world
feels impossible, which is more often than not, the hot spices of chai
soothe the rising instincts of "fight or flight" until I find my breath
and the courage for another day.

> The LORD is my caffeine,
> I shall not be weary.
> You slow my breath and restore my strength.
> Even though I walk through stress and strain,
> I do not despair for you are with me.
> Your brews and baristas, they comfort me.
> You prepare a cup before me
> in the presence of strangers.
> You anoint my life with green mermaids;
> my chai overflows.
> Surely joy and courage shall be found at the
>   bottom of each cup,
> and I shall dwell in Starbucks my whole life long.

My chai runneth over because my grief continues to runneth over
and over and over, unchecked, if disguised, into my daily life: the
guilt of a bad marriage and its lingering wounds, the sadness of love's
abandonment, the chasm of loneliness that engulfs the soul after
trauma, the weight of stresses shouldered alone.

Of all the coping mechanisms available to us through chemistry
and technology, Starbucks is arguably a harmless habit—if also a
glaringly privileged and expensive one. But when psychologists ask
about the potential harm of one's drinking habits during an intake
interview, they mean alcoholic, not caffeinated, drinks. Surely a caffeine habit isn't unhealthy. Who needs three nutritional meals per day
when you can burn through the caloric equivalent with a venti cup

of caffeinated deliciousness? Why store away the value of a month's rent for a rainy day when there's grief to be avoided and anxiety to be quelled on a daily basis? Why pray to the heavens for relief when the promises of Starbucks are available on every other city corner?

I appreciate and understand why the ancient Israelites—at a loss for direction in the wilderness, panicked by the disappearance of Moses up a clouded mountain, freed from the traumatic existence under Pharaoh only to be required by God to wander endlessly—decided to melt their jewelry and leftover lootings from Egypt to construct a golden calf for worship. There are days when I count coins just to worship again in the house of St. Arbucks. (Thankfully, now there's an app for that.) Why save patiently for the Promised Land if you're never going to get there? Of what use is freedom if survival is uncertain? Why pin your hopes on an elusive God when you can construct an illusion of assurance with your own hands?

When you're desperate for hope and normalcy, it doesn't matter if an idol is impermanent or lifeless or powerless. It doesn't matter if you know it's a false god because you ordered it on your smart-phone. When the world around you is one crisis after another, when tomorrow holds no guarantee of life or breath (let alone *new* life or *reinvigorated* breath), when God doesn't show up for you no matter your pleas, then I say, damn it all—create whatever idols you need to survive. Make a golden calf that will not leave you because you forged its altar yourself and set it on a rock. Knit your own security blanket that you can wrap around yourself at will, never needing to worry that it will be lost or taken away from you. Refill your caffeine every time the yawning bottom of the cup mocks your ability to cope. Write your own Psalm 23 if God's promises of green pastures and still waters never materialize. Call yourself "spiritual" rather than "religious" if it helps you avoid the pain of God failing to show up, even though you have said all the right prayers, burned all the right incense, donned your Sunday best, and participated faithfully in church. Hold onto an idol that can never leave you because you created it—and then recreate it with every libation you pour at the feet of a golden calf, at the tail of a green mermaid. If it reliably soothes your spirit's angst today, then love and worship it tomorrow, too. Spare yourself the trouble of grief, of doubt, of loneliness, of the pains and sins and heartaches that accompany life and faith.

I can find a Starbucks wherever I go. Whether I travel for work or move to a new state, I know that any Starbucks will make my chai latte exactly the same way. Every store will let me worship the same idol of self-sufficiency, pray for the same illusion of control, momentarily grasp the same fleeting comfort of familiarity, all for the low price of $4.45. My golden calf travels with me, and I am never alone.

That is, of course, precisely the problem with idols. Whether built out of grief or fear, in crisis or in selfishness, idols represent and perpetuate their very origins. Every sacrifice at the feet of the golden calf reminded the ancient Israelites that they were still afraid of the wilderness, still resentful at God's apparent abandonment, still suspicious that Egypt was actually better for them than the unknown Promised Land. Every cup of chai is an homage to grief and a prayer to the gods of barely coping. Every day's venti order confirms my belief that I face the world alone, that my broken reality is inadequate to meet external expectations of functioning normalcy, that God's help is unavailable to me.

Hold on. Let me refill my chai to drown out such a thought.

When God saw that the Israelites had built an idol for themselves and were burning offerings and celebrating before it, God flew into an indignant rage.

> "I will cast them out, I will wipe them from the earth, I will tear up my promises to them and start a new nation instead with Moses."[6]

But Moses dissuaded God from holy violence, suggesting the Egyptians would laugh and say that God was an evil deity who simply drew the Israelites into the wilderness to kill them. God's

---

6 Exodus 32:10, adapted.

anger cooled, but Moses went down the mountain and threw a furiously violent fit himself, commanding the sons of Levi to slay three thousand people.

> "Each of you kill your brother, your friend, and your neighbor."[7]

Then God, still determined to mete out judgment, sent a plague on the remaining Israelites who had participated in the golden calf brouhaha.

To add salt to their wounds, and as further punishment for the Israelites' idol worship, God withdrew from the people—the very reason that prompted them to build the golden calf in the first place.

> "Continue toward the land flowing with milk and honey, but I will not go with you because I'm still livid. I would destroy you if I remained among you, because you are so irritatingly stubborn."[8]

They had hoped to guarantee themselves an ever-present god with the construction of the golden calf. Instead the people caused the situation they feared most. God withdrew from them. How long would they remain abandoned this time? "Take your security blanket, your golden calf, your green mermaid, whatever your idol, and burn it; then eat the ashes. I'll check in on you again only after you've licked your plates clean of soot."

All of which is to say, if $4.45 a day doesn't dissuade me from my chai idolization, the consequences of the golden calf really should.

Idols crafted out of fear beget fear. Idols crafted out of loneliness beget loneliness. Idols built to lament the distance of God beget the distance of God. I've spent thirteen years worshiping at Starbucks;

---

[7] Exodus 32:27.

[8] Exodus 33:3, more or less.

I've been trying to quit for twelve.[9] I have journal entries that begin mournfully, "Today I had my last chai," and four hours later (not recorded in my journal, because that would be too honest) I had a fresh cup in my hand. The circle is vicious. Starbucks staves off the sense of isolation and abandonment, even as it reminds me of the same. Waiting at the counter for my drink, I am recognized by the baristas and the regulars without ever being truly known.

I try to tell myself that it's not an idol at all, that my Starbucks habit is spiritual and prayerful. Each chai is a centering prayer in the morning: "Dear Lord, help me hold it together." It's a holy moment of bringing mind, body, and spirit together into the same space. It's a confession that I am weary and that my strength alone is insufficient. It's a lament that I am broken and discouraged. And it's a psalm of praise that God's mercies are new and freshly brewed every morning.

Is it the habit that's the problem or is it the inability to release my sorrow? Can the familiar smiles of baristas be a gift, or must they heap coals upon my guilt? Can the God who detests idols and grinds them into punishment for the people's consumption also be the God who holds out grace and invites me to drink deeply? Can the God who abandoned the Israelites to their wandering and me to my pain also be the God who is unrestrained with promises of milk and honey?

I know this for sure: The vastness of God's still waters have far more room to drown my depression than a daily Starbucks cup. God's green pastures are more abundant and fruitful than an ocean of green mermaids.

> Even though I walk through stress and strain,
> I do not despair for you are with me;
> my chai overflows.

Nine pumps, no water.

---

[9] "Trying" is used loosely here.

A Six-Word Memoir

Martha

I brought some new work to my writing group, stories from my life told in miniature.

"I like it," said Barbara, whose judgment I respected. "But what is the book about? Is it a book about being adopted, or getting divorced, or is it a coming-out story?" All the writers in the group nodded, as did I. A book needs more than a genre; it needs a pithy description. I knew my answer would not meet that standard.

"It's what my life is about," I thought, "Proving I Am Not a Mistake."

I first put those words together when the Six-Word Memoir was an internet meme, one of those things people pass around and play like a game. What six words tell your life story? I thought the words through carefully, and, even though I did not like my answer, it felt truthful. I felt the pressure to prove myself as an adopted daughter so I would somehow fit into the family story. I felt it as a person who lost her social status after divorce. I felt it after the belated recognition of my orientation, unsure of the response of friends both queer and straight.

If it's true that we form our earliest impressions of God through our relationships with our parents, that might explain why I instinctively think that God (the Mother) wants it done right while God (the Father) hopes for a lot but expects to be disappointed. When your parents give you those messages, you know which one you have to work harder to suit. I veered back and forth between the two, trying to prove myself and figuring there was not much point to trying. Sometimes I knew the truth that God loved me just as I was, knowing where I had come from, with the bizarre mixture of nature and nurture and self-work my life expressed. At other times I believed the lie that God would only love me if I proved I was worth it.

In my twenties, just before I moved from Virginia to Maine, I sought information about my birth parents. The law in Virginia allowed an adoptee to see redacted records. On a dreary day, I drove I-64 East from Charlottesville to Richmond, to find an office park where the physical records were kept. I received a copy of the microfiche records with the identifying information cut out of the physical pages. I could see my birthmother's birthdate; it was the same month and day as my adoptive mother's, who was sixteen years older. The file contained paragraph-long biographical statements and a story told by a social worker. Some of it had been passed along to my adoptive parents, but not all.[1] Reading it in the 1980s, I could feel the "wholesomeness-washing": the attempt to make the situation sound bad enough for the birth mother to not keep her baby, but not so bad that the adoptive parents would not want the child.

"Unwanted, but Wantable Enough for Some."

That sounds terrible. Let's forget that one.

My dad stepped in to help me find out more. Adopting had been his idea, a subject he raised one morning over breakfast after he and my mother had been married ten years. Because she had been an adoption worker prior to their marriage, he suggested she call someone at her old office and see about getting a baby. I believe this story, because my parents told it to me separately with a remarkable similarity of details. We learned that the original, more detailed files still existed, and were kept in the Social Service offices in my hometown, less than ten blocks from my childhood home. I got permission to call a social worker who looked over the file. She found a handwritten local phone number at the top of the page, and the

---

[1] And only some of it proved true.

name of a woman next to it. She called the number and reached my birth mother's aunt, who still lived at the same address. My great aunt agreed to reach out to my birth mother, and after several phone calls between various parties, we talked and agreed to meet.

Her story is hers to tell. I will only tell you the parts that, having heard them, now feel like mine. I was conceived the summer after her freshman year in college. She kept me a secret as long as she could, camouflaged by the girdle-dominant styles of the 1960–61 school year, until her mother finally told her she looked like she was pregnant. I was another person's un-confessable predicament.

"My Mother Could Not Confess Me."

I was a mistake for my birth mother. For a long time I thought knowing more about where I came from might make me feel better, but it didn't. The story had neither romance nor tragedy, just two young human beings having sex and an outcome—me—they did not share. I have met my birth mother's family, including my half brother. The man who provided the other half of my DNA doesn't know I exist. My birth mother and I once drove by his house and saw him in the yard; when we turned the corner there was a snake in the road. Every now and then I look him up to see if he is still alive. It's easier to track erstwhile family members in this era of Facebook. He has a wife and a daughter and a grandchild. Although my birth mother told me I have the same slim gap between my front teeth, I don't see any resemblance between my people and his. Long before I might ever think about contacting him, I remember that snake.

"In Which I Avoid the Snake"—that's not a fully realized memoir, but it's oddly satisfying. Snakes are not a typical feature of my storytelling. I did once not buy a house because I saw a tiny snake in the side yard, but the fauna in my style of parables tend to be dogs, or occasionally cats. Jesus tended toward flora in his illustrations: seeds, fig trees, mustard bushes, vineyards, and wheat.

> He put before them another parable: "The kingdom of heaven may be compared to someone

who sowed good seed in his field; but while every-
body was asleep, an enemy came and sowed weeds
among the wheat, and then went away. So when
the plants came up and bore grain, then the weeds
appeared as well. And the slaves of the householder
came and said to him, 'Master, did you not sow
good seed in your field? Where, then, did these
weeds come from?' He answered, 'An enemy has
done this.' The slaves said to him, 'Then do you
want us to go and gather them?' But he replied,
'No; for in gathering the weeds you would uproot
the wheat along with them. Let both of them grow
together until the harvest; and at harvest time I
will tell the reapers, Collect the weeds first and
bind them in bundles to be burned, but gather the
wheat into my barn.'"[2]

Jesus's listeners would have grasped the agricultural details as quickly
as my last congregation did my plentiful baseball references. The
weed he mentions, a darnel, looked so much like wheat that the two
could not be differentiated until they were fully grown.

"Let them grow together until the harvest."

I know God loves us all, and that "all" includes me. I am well
aware of, and have spent many therapeutic dollars to ponder, the
ways in which my early life experiences contributed to my sense of
never being enough. It manifests in ways large and small: thinking
I'm beholden to others for actions they don't remember; assuming
I ought not take up space in their lives; working to perform acts
of kindness that go beyond any reasonable requirements; thinking
I must always put others first, even when they don't think so themselves. In every decade of my life, my worry of unworthiness appears
in some new form. I have long said I don't believe in a devil who

---

2 Matthew 13:24–30.

personifies evil, but there surely seems to be some enemy at work sowing anxiety.

When my son Peter was a tween, he went through a picky-eating phase until he saw an older cousin refusing food at a family party. He said to me later, "I don't want to be that guy." I watched him use that reasoning throughout his teenage years to correct himself, most of the time by comparing himself, not to an actual person, but to a type.

"Don't Want to Be That Guy."

As much as I chuckled over the idea the first time he said it, his eleven-year-old wisdom stayed with me. There may be some things we cannot change, but we can shift what is in our minds. If I don't want to be that woman, that person, who keeps circling back around to the same old trouble, I have to find a way to be more patient with myself. I need to let the crop grow right alongside the weeds and not tear it all out of the ground, but it is hard to wait and watch. For years, in talking about my work in ministry, I said I wanted to be useful on behalf of Jesus Christ. Sometimes I said "I just want to be useful," which carries a different nuance, as if I were asking for something very small, the crumb of having God put me to work in some useful way. Over those same years, I often told the story about my Grandmother Spong snapping me to attention with the caution, "Make yourself useful as well as decorative."

"Be Useful as Well as Decorative."

"Useful on Behalf of Jesus Christ."

These are the same. I believed that usefulness mattered the most. People who were useful could not be a mistake. God wanted them for something.

When I moved to Pennsylvania, I no longer had work to do in a church and it seemed uncertain when I would again. Yes, a job would have been good, and, yes, my gifts and training suited me to pastoral ministry, but my feelings of angst went deeper than worrying about a place to go to work. Being a pastor and serving a church meant being useful; it amounted to an assurance that God valued me. How could I prove I was not a mistake if God did not want me? Whatever part of me still felt inadequate, unwanted, and just not right for anyone had an appallingly transactional view of God. I felt I had to be useful to be acceptable. A good way to test a feeling like that, especially when you have made God part of it, is to ask yourself whether you would ever believe it applied to another person. I would never do that to someone else.

Last summer I went to a national church meeting as a visitor and sat in on one of the business sessions. A resolution was offered, entitled "The Disparity of Rights of Adoptees to Access Birth Certificates for Adults." State laws vary. Adoptees' access to information depends on the state in which they were born. The resolution only asked for education: that the Church would pay attention to the inequity present in the disparity. The committee of delegates that had studied the resolution came to the general session sharply divided. The testimony both for and against painted birth mothers and adoptees as likely bad actors: the mothers did not care about their children; the children became adults who might stalk and harass the women who gave them life. We heard from adoptive mothers and sisters, from advocates for birth mothers, from pastors who care. We never heard a word from an adopted person. I wondered who else in the room was trying not to curse out loud, was wishing it were over, was not caring how it turned out as long as the room could return to the normal sense of boredom that comes with doing denominational business. I wondered who else longed for a space where we were not the unspeaking focus of attention. The lives of adoptees— our lives—sounded like the weeds, being tolerated only to spare the wheat for the harvest.

The parables Jesus wove out of the places he went and the people he met have as many interpretations as that resolution, even when they both seem obvious on first reading. I love to play with the parables, considering different ways of understanding. What if some of us are weeds and some are wheat? Are the weeds going to hell? What if we are all both wheat and weeds? What if Jesus was wondering how his life and his ministry would be sorted out in the end? To show that the kingdom of heaven was not as simple as sorting out bad things from good,

> He told them another parable: "The kingdom of heaven is like yeast that a woman took and mixed in with three measures of flour until all of it was leavened."[3]

Instead of being a bad thing like the weeds, the yeast spreads through the flour and changes it for the better—makes it more useful, if you will—but, in the process, becomes something you cannot see.

I have the baby book my mother wrote out in her beautiful cursive. On one of the first pages, there are spaces for national and local headlines on the day the baby was born. I came to my parents as a two-week-old. In that time Alan Shepard had become the first American to achieve earth orbit. Her local headline? "The Spongs Have Adopted a Baby Girl." While they did not receive the same global interest as an astronaut, my father was the state senator, and, in their circles, everyone knew how long they had been married without having children. Close friends had counted the months that became a year while they waited for word about a baby.

When I talked with my dad about whether or not to meet my birth mother and told him what I had learned about her life, I wondered how he felt about the next step of contacting her, which was made possible by his help. My mother was hurt and could not talk about it much; perhaps he added to her hurt by giving me assistance. They adopted in an era when some blamed the birth parents for any bad character seen in the children. We were all potential weeds planted by enemies. That day, when I saw the unusual sight of tears in his eyes, I leaned in closer to hear his soft drawl.

"Well, Maw-thuh, I'd like to think I'm willing to take credit not just for your good qualities, but for your bad ones, too."

"I Had a Really Good Daddy."

---

[3] Matthew 13:33.

My relationship with my birth mother felt difficult and tenuous, just like my relationship with my mother. Maybe that was always going to be the story of my life. My values, my tastes, my amusements were all Spong. I learned to love books and baseball, the beach and Benny Goodman. I learned to value people of all kinds and believe all people were equal because my dad did, and that he believed all those things because Jesus did. I was his daughter. I am his daughter. That can't have been a mistake.

> Jesus told the crowds all these things in parables; without a parable he told them nothing. This was to fulfill what had been spoken through the prophet:
> "I will open my mouth to speak in parables;
> I will proclaim what has been hidden from the foundation of the world."[4]

"Yeast Mixed with Flour Yields Bread." "Enemy Sows Weeds in Wheat Field." "Don't Pick Wheat before It's Full-Grown."

These six-word stories are not wrong, but they give us only the barest understanding of Jesus's parables, broadcasting sound bites rather than invitations to explore more deeply. We have learned to assume that a restless world demands *Short Attention Span Theater.* So much of what we see now scrolls by in Facebook posts and tweets and news alerts; reality gets pared down to an anxious buzz and fractious responses. In too many places we try to squeeze ourselves into a limited character count. We lose the depth of the story and with it the truth. Thank God, God has a longer attention span than we do. God has the patience to let the story play out in as many words, letters, spaces, ellipses, and exclamation points as we need to live our full lives.

"God Waits to See What Matures."

I still fall into feeling that I need to prove myself—to other

---

[4] Matthew 13:34–35.

people and to God—in order to win favor. This failure of faith will probably never leave me completely. It is so much a part of who I am that there is no way to tell for sure which stalk is a weed and which is the wheat. I will keep working at it, not because God won't love me unless I do, but because I love God and want to do better in my response to God's love for me.

"Loved by God. Make No Mistake."

When I Look at the Heavens

Rachel

I want bouquets of flowers. Not roses—too cliché. Not often—just once in a while to surprise me. I want a foot massage for no particular reason or for those moments when life leaves me at a loss for words. I want someone else to cook sometimes. I want a sounding board, a listening ear, an external perspective to counterbalance the maddening echoes in my own head.

I want a cup brimming with joyful companionship.

During my teenage years, the Church had good news for romantic dreams like mine: "Stay celibate, love Jesus, and the perfect God-chosen spouse will appear in your life." It was the Christianized fairy tale, or maybe the Disney-fied theology, conveyed between the lines of devotional materials that strove to temper teenagers' sexual desire with a romanticized relationship with Jesus: "Jesus knows you're prettier than the lilies. Jesus knows every hair on your head and has a crown to set upon it. Jesus will never leave or disappoint you. Fall in love with Jesus while you wait for God to bless you with your very own Christian Prince Charming: your soul's match, your heart's desire, your chosen one."

The fine print included a caveat: "If you make Jesus cry because of your sinful behavior, then all promises for holy matchmaking are null and void."

I have probably made Jesus cry too often to win the romantic prize at the end of the faith rainbow. I broke curfew in high school, daring an extra five or ten minutes in the car with a good Christian boy. I got tattoos in college and cut my hair short—the faithless horror! After college I moved from rural Pennsylvania to the big city of Washington, D.C. and, one year later, I gave birth to a son . . . wait for it . . . out of wedlock. Without intending to, I had taken the list of "thou shalt nots" from my teenage devotionals and checked off every item as a "thou shalt."

Those same teen devotionals warned that my social sins revealed my spiritual starvation as measured by the wholesome standards of Group Publishing, Focus on the Family, and the like. To feed my apparent starvation, therefore, I ate heartily from the banquet table of Good Christian Girl Guilt. Good Christian Girl Guilt was the meager meal available to those of us who made Jesus cry, whose sins meant that our Fairy God-the-Father would offer us grace, but never a happy ending. The theological irony was clear: Grace put you right with God for eternity, but your guilt forever disqualified you from the fairy tale.

If the heteronormative fulfillment of righteous faith was supposed to be a magical marriage between a Prince Charming and a Cinderella who prayed together, those of us who missed the ball were sent back to the ash pit to dig around for whatever embers might still be coaxed into a fire. By then, we were no longer errant teenagers but adults trying to find our way back into the Christian fold of social "normalcy," believing it was necessary for our salvation to do so. After my divorce, I found an ember who saw himself as a fiery Prince Charming. He was willing to help me see myself as a still-faithful

Cinderella. He said he didn't mind my messy life. He said I was lucky to have him because most men would look at me and conclude that I was all used up. He said it was okay that I had missed the ball because it meant he could rescue me from the ash heap. And since Good Christian Girl Guilt taught me that I should accept whatever guy appointed himself as God's gift for me, I said yes.

I really wanted to hold the cup of joy and companionship for a change. I wanted to set down my cup of single motherhood, because although I loved parenting on my own, the cup itself was often and painfully met with righteous judgment by the world and especially the Church. Still, scrounging at the table of Good Christian Girl Guilt just to raise a cup of joy was a trade-off that depended on shame. Not every happiness is worth its price. When, at last, I shed my Prince Charming and my teenage-rotted visions of a romantic Christian fairy tale, not only did I stop believing in holy happy endings, I stopped believing that Jesus cared at all about my romantic life or its prospects for satisfaction. Baby. Bathwater. If Jesus knew the hairs on my head, then I had to believe realistically that Jesus knew the hairs on everyone's heads, yet this holy familiarity wasn't yielding a global harvest of joy. It was simply a matter of looking at the world around me to notice that most people held cups of sorrow and struggle that they would rather relinquish.

Maybe you've noticed, too, that the world is raging and devouring itself: wars and rumors of wars, devastating storms and fierce wildfires, corruption and oppression, pollution and poverty. Even if I *do* warrant individual attention from the Most High God, from the Powerful Creator of vast galaxies, it seems the starting point for God's intervention cannot possibly be my love life. Probably not yours either, but I'll leave that question to you and God. Why would God Almighty spend an iota of eternity trying to find my next romantic partner, when kids around the world go to sleep hungry? How can Jesus have any spare time to set me up on blind dates when racism is bleeding all over his hands—from my city, where a boy was shot and killed by police at the playground, to the city where men with tiki torches surrounded a church full of people praying against racism?

> When I look at your heavens, the work of your fingers,
> the moon and the stars that you have established,
> what are human beings that you are mindful of them,
> mortals that you care for them?[5]

The psalmist's question is often read with a tone of wonder and gratitude: "Wow! The universe is vast and stunning, yet still God knows and cares for humanity." To the contrary, I hear Psalm 8 as practical and resigned: "Look at everything you can do, God. There's simply no reason for human beings to be worth your time and attention, despite our needy demands for your care." If, against all odds, God cares intimately for humanity, such holy affections seem best understood through Psalm 8's rationale for why God would give a damn—because humanity has been given the holy assignment of tending Creation.

> "You have given them dominion
> over the works of your hands;
> you have put all things under their feet,
> all sheep and oxen,
> and also the beasts of the field,
> the birds of the air, and the fish of the sea,
> whatever passes along the paths of the seas."[6]

The psalmist invokes gratitude for God's attention, not to encourage our fantasies of God's swooning love and propensity for happy endings, but to remind us of God's assigned purpose for humanity. From the origins of Creation, God shaped dust into reflections of God's image and breathed life into them, in order to set them in the world to care for it. They—we—were crafted to be faithful coworkers, not glass-slipper dancers.

In other words, or so I tell myself, Cinderella wasn't meant for princes at all, no matter how charming. She was meant to sing with

---

[5] Psalm 8:3–4.
[6] Psalm 8:6–8.

the birds, to care for the barn animals, to tend the fires so that she could cook a hot meal for neighbors who were sick. I guess Disney actually got that part right. The goodness that is worth seeking in life is the worship of God and the care of Creation—neighbor and stranger working together in community for the sake of the fox and foal, city and desert, soaring sequoia and winding river. God does not promise happily-ever-afters, at least not in this life. This is not the bitter wisdom of rejected Cinderellas; it is the patient wisdom of stargazers and dreamers and exalted heroes of faith.

Abraham gazed at the heavens and heard God's promise that his descendants would outnumber the stars,[7] yet at the time of Abraham's death, he could count the number of sons on his hands and feet—a constellation of children, perhaps, but hardly a galaxy.[8] God's promise was unfulfilled in Abraham's lifetime. Moses spent decades chasing pillars of fire and cloud through the wilderness in pursuit of the Promised Land, only to die within sight of that glorious fulfillment.[9] Simeon and Anna dreamed of seeing the day when the Kingdom of God was fulfilled on earth; instead they got to hold a baby.[10] Jesus himself asked for a happy ending—"Remove this cup from me"[11]—but still the soldiers came.

Hannah was diligent in her prayers, asking God year after year after year for a son. Heartbroken that she had not yet conceived with her husband Elkanah, Hannah poured out her prayer in the temple and placed her shame before God for redemption. So intense were her prayers that the priest Eli became annoyed. He thought she must be drunk to lack decorum in such a public place, so he pulled her aside to suggest that she was making a scene and should stop embarrassing herself. But if great men of faith could cry out to God in

---

[7] Genesis 15:5.

[8] Ishmael, Isaac, Zimran, Jokshan, Medan, Midian, Ishbak, Shuah, born to Hagar, Sarah, and Keturah. There were also sons (uncounted) born to Abraham's concubines. (Genesis 25:1–6).

[9] Deuteronomy 32:52.

[10] Luke 2:25–38.

[11] Luke 22:42.

public and plead for God's grace and miracles, Hannah believed she could do the same. "I have been speaking out of my great anxiety and vexation."[12] When Eli blessed her prayers and Hannah gave birth to a son, even then the fulfillment of her dream was not intended for her own joy but for God's purposes, and Hannah gave her son Samuel to the temple to be trained as a priest in Eli's care.

> With the heavens established to sing your praises,
> with the moon and the stars created to provide you joy,
> what is humanity to you, O God, except coworkers for the
> sake of Creation?

Lo and behold, Psalm 8 sounds remarkably similar to my "justification by works" German sensibility. No wonder I'm single. There's not a romantic whim in my body, and I believe in a God who calls us to work rather than pleasure. I may want flowers, but if someone actually gave me a bouquet I would need to clean the house in order to put the flowers on display properly. If someone took the time to offer a foot massage, I would withdraw and make excuses for my calloused feet. If someone offered to cook dinner, I would insist on grocery shopping and then washing the dishes.

Clearly I could use some divine intervention in the dating game, but still I maintain that God has far better things to do than play matchmaker. There are galaxies to coordinate in their dance, the nighttime moon and daytime star to keep in their courses. There are babes to be coached in prophecy, and infants to be charged with silencing injustice.[13] There are angelic choirs to rehearse the songs of God's glory. In the midst of it all, my one little heart's happy ending is insignificant. And whether it's the humility of mature faith or the unconscious lingering of Good Christian Girl Guilt that puts me in my place within the grand scheme of Creation, the result is as it should be: with God doing God's business and me doing my part.

---

[12] 1 Samuel 1:16.
[13] Psalm 8:2.

The people I admire most in life are those who do not chase happily-ever-afters because they are committed to being present with and working faithfully alongside others, whether in marriage or in friendship, among neighbors and strangers, in person or online. The people who remind me that God's promises are not fairy tales are those who choose love every day, not because it's romantic but because it keeps them rooted in community—because it keeps them rooted in God. The cup that I need God to take from me isn't singleness or even loneliness, but rather the cup of despair that tempts me to withdraw to my own personal ash heap just because I missed the ball once upon a time.

Moving On

Rachel

One of the treatments for post-traumatic stress disorder (PTSD) is prolonged exposure therapy: the guided experience of retelling or re-experiencing a traumatic event until the memory loses its sting and becomes normalized among other memories. Which is how I ended up in a psychologist's office, describing the long-ago experience of seeing a black Mercury Mountaineer in my rearview mirror on a road trip through the Catskills on I-87: the panic that flooded me as that SUV followed my little Corolla for miles, the struggle to keep my voice calm and light for my children who were with me, the desperate effort to control my speed so that I wasn't close enough for the Mountaineer's driver to see in my car yet I could still maintain visual confirmation of the vehicle's location.

I had last seen that Mountaineer on a September day—was it two years before that alarmed trip up I-87 or only one or maybe three?—when my then-husband drove away from our Maryland apartment, presumably going to work, but actually leaving. Leaving the country. Leaving me and our children, who were one and four at the time. Fleeing the inevitability of his imprisonment. Fleeing with a hundred dollars cash he had overdrawn from our bank account.

Initially the county detectives were interested in the missing Mountaineer and its owner. I met with them for an official interview.

Did I know where the vehicle was? No.

Did I know my then-husband's intended destination? No.

Would I take their business cards and contact them with any new information? Certainly.

I finally learned of the Mountaineer's location when the car loan company called several months later to let me know they had found the vehicle in New York City. I had not been looking for it. They were in the process of towing it.

Did I know how it got there and did I want to reclaim it? No and no.

They were welcome to keep it, which they did. They were welcome to not call me again; they were less inclined to agree on that point. We had many long conversations, the loan company and I, about the financial responsibility for the Mountaineer until finally I stopped taking their calls.

The disappearance of his vehicle—first from Maryland and then from New York—meant that he was gone, simultaneously creating an enormous relief and a frightening new world for me. I was thrust into single motherhood, but, for the first time, I was able to regain control of my family's well-being. My not-yet-ex disappeared as effectively as his Mountaineer, going off the grid for legal reasons. I took the kids and myself off the grid as much as I could possibly manage for safety reasons. I changed our address to a post office box and told only a few people where we were moving. We moved twice more within that first year, never announcing our new location, never publicizing the address. I chose only apartments that had two sets of locked doors between my family and the rest of the world, preferably not on the ground floor. The worst of these apartments had an infestation of roaches in the kitchen, rats that governed the backyard where the trash cans were kept, and a pot-smoking neighbor whose late night deals sometimes meant that people accidentally knocked on my door at 2 a.m. But it had two sets of locked doors.

I tried not to sleep during those first few years, dozing in front of the television's blue screen through the night, keeping the volume low so I could listen for suspicious sounds inside or outside the apartment. I double-checked the locks, not only on doors but also on windows. I opened closet doors to make sure only coats were inside. Over the years of relocations, if I couldn't find an apartment with multiple locked layers, I set ridiculous "booby traps" at night for lack of an alarm system: toys scattered on the stairs, for example, to increase that odds that someone would make noise if they broke into the house and tried to sneak up to the bedrooms. I never told people I did these things, of course; the stresses of trauma look outlandish to others.

The sight of the Mountaineer barreling north on I-87 triggered my worst nightmare: the possibility that my ex would return to pursue me and the kids. My body's tension could have been plucked like a string as I gripped the wheel. Every effort I had made to protect us, all of the energy I had spent on fear since his departure, was to no avail if he had zeroed in on us while we were traveling to one of the places that I considered safest: the home of friends in upstate New York. There should have been no reason why he would know that I would be on that particular highway on that particular day. There was no reason for him even to be in the country. The official police report said they had lost track of him. The unofficial family report said he had moved to another continent.

I tried to reason with myself as I watched my speed and kept an eye on the Mountaineer. Maybe it was sheer coincidence that we were on the same highway. Maybe he hadn't seen me. Had he turned to look at my Corolla when we first passed him, when I first realized that the SUV might be his? Maybe it wasn't even him. I had not gotten a good look at the driver. The man behind the wheel was his height, but my brain couldn't grasp any other details of the driver's face. I reminded myself that the vehicle had been repossessed by the loan company. It was reasonable to conclude that they would have resold it. Maybe there was more than one black Mercury Mountaineer in the eastern U.S. In the wake of trauma, fear disrupts reality, and I could not grasp the possibility that other Mountaineers might be on the road.

The time on the highway seemed endless. Did I have enough gas to outlast him if he didn't exit before I did? I couldn't take my

planned exit if he was still behind me, of course. I wracked my brain
to remember how well I knew any of the other exits. I had not yet
gotten passports for the kids, so following I-87 all the way north
into Canada wasn't an option. I would need to refuel before then
anyway. After an eternity at seventy-five miles per hour, he exited.
I didn't stop studying my rear view mirror until I left the highway
two hours later.

Back in the psychologist's office, I was asked to focus on the SUV.
What other memories did I associate with it? What other details
about it did I remember?

It seems that we took a family trip in the SUV years earlier. I
remembered riding in the black vehicle, him on the driver's side,
the kids in their car seats, a sewing project on my lap. I described
the scene to the psychologist. There was no tension in that memory,
only a family driving on a sunny day to visit the in-laws. I smiled to
remember that we didn't always fight, that sometimes he laughed,
that sometimes he made the kids laugh instead of cry. Several days
after describing that pleasant scene to my therapist, I realized there
was no way it could have happened. The family trip I remembered
occurred a year prior to his purchase of the Mountaineer. Memory
fooled me as much as it haunted me.

I appreciated that the psychologist was pursuing a therapeutic
goal when she asked me to return again and again to the image of
the Mountaineer, but I wanted to borrow Hagar's words and shout
at the therapist: "Don't make me look on the death."[1] If pain and
sorrow were inevitable, if trauma had to be endured, I didn't want to
look directly at it.

Hagar had spent all her energy across the years keeping a close
eye on her son, Ishmael, who was born as Abraham's first son but
never received by Sarah as her own child. It was Sarah's decision that
Abraham should take her slave girl Hagar as his "wife,"[2] with the

---

[1] Genesis 21:16.
[2] Genesis 16:3 uses "wife," although it was a forced arrangement for Hagar to bear
children.

intention that Sarah would claim any resulting children as her own. But Sarah rejected Ishmael and punished Hagar, so Hagar watched Ishmael closely—guarding him against slight, encouraging his bond with Abraham, striving to ensure that Ishmael would not be as easily dismissed as she had been. She wanted him to be known fully and only as Abraham's son and heir, even if she could not escape her status as slave.

Hagar's worst nightmare came true when Sarah conceived and gave birth to Isaac. Any begrudging acknowledgement that Sarah had granted Ishmael as the firstborn son of Abraham was now gone. To Sarah, Ishmael was only the son of a slave, and she demanded that Abraham cast Hagar and Ishmael out from the camp. The bread and the water with which Abraham equipped them didn't last long in the wilderness. When it seemed that Ishmael might die of thirst, Hagar made him comfortable as best she could in the shade of a bush and then pleaded with God:

> "After all that I have seen, after all my loving vigilance over Ishmael across these years, do not make me watch his death."[3]

What was there to be gained by searing Ishmael's dying breath into her memory? Why would God compound her trauma by making her listen to her son's cries from dire thirst, and then to his silence as he faded from life? How could there ever be enough medicines and diagnoses and therapy couches to ease her memory of that moment, to lessen the pain of knowing that she had not been able to rescue her son from this death?

That an angel appeared to Hagar to rescue her and her son from death does not redeem God, for me, in this story. How loudly did Hagar have to cry and shout to the heavens, how near to death did Ishmael have to hover before God remembered to listen? How many days did Hagar and Ishmael have to linger and drink from

---

[3] Genesis 21:16, adapted.

that divinely-appeared well before their strength returned? And how many days earlier in the journey could God have pointed out the well for Hagar to avoid the trauma of believing that she would have to bury her child? That God heard their cries only meant that God let them cry in the first place.

> "God said to Abraham, 'Do not be distressed because of the boy and because of your slave woman; whatever Sarah says to you [about casting them out], do as she tells you.'"[4]

How does this holy advice uphold the reputation of a God whose heart inclines toward the oppressed, whose spirit holds the wicked accountable?

> We have waited.
> We have hoped.
> Perhaps now
> at long last
> God will answer
> the generations
> who have cried.
> Perhaps.
> But here—
> here is a
> shoulder
> for comfort
> until God
> comes. Unless
> God doesn't come.
> Unless the desert
> never blooms.

---

[4] Genesis 21:12.

Unless the streams
never bubble in song.
What if. . . ?
What if never?
Cry, creation, cry
and say farewell.
Salvation isn't
coming for you.[5]

Do not make those who are most pained and grieved see death unfold before them, O God. Do not make Hagar watch her own son die. Do not make me relive trauma and pretend that it is relieved.

More than a decade after my fear of the Mountaineer had faded, a message came from my sister-in-law. She wrote to tell me that my ex-husband was marrying an American. But I misread the e-mail. I thought she was telling me that my ex-husband was returning to America. My body froze immediately and my mind raced. How quickly could I get home from work to pull my kids out of school? Where was he most likely to show up? We couldn't move again; I had promised the kids that we would remain rooted long enough for them to finish high school. Could we at least get out of town for a few days, or take an extended vacation? Traveling might not be the best option. What security measures had I allowed to lapse over the years that I could put back in place in case he tried to find us? I had become careless and no longer used a post office box for our mailing address. Would he be able to search online for our home address? The kids usually walked home from school as part of their daily routines; perhaps I should start picking them up again.

I spent a full fifteen minutes in panic and shock before I reread the e-mail and realized my error. He wasn't coming. I tried to breathe. He wasn't coming. I didn't have to rush home to the kids. I could

5 Rachel G. Hackenberg, excerpt of "Advent: Goodbye," December 6, 2016, rachelhackenberg.com.

see them at the end of their school day as usual. He wasn't coming.
It was okay. He wasn't coming.

> Do not make us live out our nightmares, O God.
> Do not make us watch death.
> Rescue us—soon!—with a wellspring of peace,
>   an oasis of hope.
> Like fresh water on parched tongues, wash over
>   our stresses and traumas,
> Most Merciful God, and strengthen us to carry
>   on without fear.

Not Okay

Martha

Neither of us sent Christmas cards the year Kathryn and I
got married. Our wedding was December 30, a celebration
aligned with the madness of packing up and closing on my house
in Maine after a three day honeymoon. Six weeks later, after we had
photos from the big day, I sat at my desk and surfed from Snapfish
to Shutterfly to Paper Culture, dropping our favorites into layouts,
looking for one that allowed the flexibility to announce our marriage, indicate my new address, and drop news that would come as
an unpleasant surprise for some people.

Our wedding invitations had been fabulous, designed by my
soon-to-be sister-in-law, with elegant reply cards. We wanted everything about the ceremony, the reception, and the peripherals to seem
as grown-up as possible. The invited group was small, just the closest
family and some dear friends who supported us along the way. We

let everyone know as soon as we started planning so they could save
the date.

I contacted my brother via e-mail. It felt less awkward than a
phone call. We had had a very uncomfortable conversation earlier
that year when I was on college visits with my daughter, Lucy. I've
always admired people who can play it cool about what other people
think and just be who they are and never answer questions. I am
not one of those people. I tend to over-explain as much as I over-
prepare, for my own comfort and for the sake of anyone else I think
I can make comfortable, but I did not know how to do that when it
came time to come out to my brother. Somehow in the gap between
my self-realization, sharing with my kids and closest friends, and the
decision Kathryn and I made to move toward getting married, there
had been no opportunity to talk with him.

I didn't set out to have an emotional distance from my family,
but the death of our parents and the geographic distance between
us meant we would have needed to really want the connection and
would have needed to work on maintaining it. The more time that
passed, the less I heard from family on my mother's side. I had a life
in Maine, and my brother and cousins had theirs in Virginia. On
my father's side, I had kept in touch with Cousin Jack, who always
asked if I had talked to my brother. My brother had done a better
job making birthday and holiday phone calls than I ever did, but
our conversations felt perfunctory, a duty crossed off a list. At no
time had he suggested getting together in person. The last visit I had
made to Virginia seven years earlier gave me information that seemed
pertinent now: My sister-in-law had spoken openly against same-sex
relationships, raising the topic herself for no particular reason.

My brilliant idea was to take Lucy to visit my alma mater,
William and Mary, as part of her eleventh-grade college tour. We
would use her spring break to visit Vassar, stop in Pennsylvania to
visit Dickinson College, pick up Kathryn and her seven-year-old son,
Will, and then swing down through Virginia before coming back via
Bryn Mawr and Haverford. Our side trip did not make sense without
the incentive to see my brother. Maybe incentive is not the right

word. I needed an excuse because I wanted to tell him in person, so I made the arrangements and added that I would be traveling with a friend.

Lucy and I left Maine, accompanied by our rescue Bernese Mountain Dog, Hoagie. While walking him in the parking lot of the La Quinta in Danbury, Connecticut, I got a call from my brother. He wanted to firm up our plans for later in the week, and he particularly wanted to arrange to have dinner without my friend. Shit got real there in the parking lot, as I juggled a poop bag, a 130-pound dog, and the truth.

"She's the reason I'm coming to see you. She's the special person in my life," I said. "I'm coming there so you can meet her."

"Okay," he said. Then he said it ten more times. "Okay, okay, okay, okay, okay." A pause. "Okay, okay, okay, okay, okay."

At his invitation, we met at his house, where I saw his half of the family pictures and the furniture we had divided after our dad died fifteen years earlier. I saw a painting by the same artist whose work hung in my living room. I saw the desk where my mother used to respond to invitations and fill out the Social Security forms for our maid. Kathryn told me later I had unconsciously reached to caress a polished wardrobe. The time that had gone by meant these things felt less a real part of my life somehow, like representations in a beautifully kept museum. They were pieces of a life I did not have anymore. I had become a stranger.

His wife met us for dinner after work. She was the wild card in my mind. She asked if I was planning to move to Pennsylvania to be with Kathryn. I acknowledged that we were talking about it, and she nodded. She said the next time we came to Williamsburg, we should stay with them. I thought things went well, but escaping without a scene may be a pretty low standard for family relationships.

Mark says Jesus called his disciples together on a mountaintop, after which:

> [Jesus] went home; and the crowd came together
> again, so that they could not even eat. When his

family heard it, they went out to restrain him, for people were saying, "He has gone out of his mind."[6]

The home Jesus returned to was not his hometown of Nazareth but his adopted home of Capernaum, the home of Peter and Andrew. I've always thought it was funny that he got them to drop their nets and follow, but they almost immediately took him home for dinner. Word got out that he made regular returns to this home base, and that's where his family came looking for him, all the way from Nazareth. I can picture Peter, or perhaps one of the Sons of Thunder, keeping an eye on the scene, murmuring, "Okay. Okay, okay, okay."

The family was outside, muttering that Jesus was out of his mind, or that people thought he was, which was just as bad. Then the scribes entered the picture and said, "He has Beelzebub, and by the ruler of the demons he casts out demons."[7] Out of his mind and possessed by a demon, and not just any demon; the scribes thought Jesus had great and terrible powers. He did, although not from the place they imagined. So often we just want people to stop being their unrestrained selves. People being who they really are can be difficult, stressful, embarrassing. It was for Jesus's family. But Jesus had a sermon, and he preached the hell out of it.

You are confused about who has the power, he said. Don't call me names, and don't condemn yourselves further with poor spiritual logic. Know who I am. Calling me what I am not—that's the unforgivable sin. Jesus may have rarely been straightforward, teaching as he did with stories and images, but he was always real.[8]

I can't say I was real with my brother and his family. Maybe I should have said something sooner, but the trouble was I didn't know how to describe myself. Lesbian? I felt too inexperienced. Bisexual? I could see why people might assume that, but it wasn't true. Queer?

---

[6] Mark 3:20–21.

[7] Mark 3:22.

[8] Paraphrasing Mark 3:23–30

I came to like the term later, but at the time it sounded shocking. I wanted something safer. "Not straight." "Loves Kathryn." "Um."

Okay. Okay, okay, okay, okay, okay.

When I emailed the "save the date," my brother said he would come to my wedding, and I believed him. He said, in fact, he would come with his family. Months later, as we counted out seats at the reception tables, we waited for his official response, needing a specific number from him. I finally asked about his plans via another e-mail, and, while he did not confirm he would be there, he let me know at most there would be two or three people out of the possible five. We moved names around on our seating plan, and sent out another invitation to the first couple on our version of a waiting list.

My home office in Portland was the kitchen table. I had a special tree I could see from that window, a flowering tree that yielded unexpected apples. That fall, I knew I was watching the leaves fall from it for the last time as I made notes for sermons and prepared lectures for a class I taught, and as I refreshed my e-mail again and again for news from my realtor and my seamstress and my brother. Endings and beginnings bend close together with their sentiments of "never again" and "only this once," a last look weighted differently than a first kiss even when both prove momentous. Over that summer, Kathryn took Will on the Sidewinder, a roller coaster at Hersheypark that pulls riders up and lets them go through a series of loops, then pulls them up a parallel track and lets them go again, this time in reverse. "This is okay," they said to reassure each other as the crank first pulled the cars to the top. "It's okay." As soon as the cars clanked into place, even before the drop, they yelled, "Not okay! Not okay!"

The closer the wedding got, the more okay/not okay I became. My brother knew better than to RSVP at the last minute. Not only were we raised better, but he worked in the hospitality industry and knew we needed numbers for the restaurant. Three days before the wedding, he called to offer a handful of excuses about his family's schedule, his work, and his wife's. We learned he also called Cousin Jack, who told him that when you have that many excuses, none of them is the real reason. In their conversation, the truth became clear. His wife did not like it that two women were getting married. Not okay. Cousin Jack still urged me to stay in touch with my brother.

> Then his mother and his brothers came; and standing outside, they sent to him and called him. A crowd was sitting around him; and they said to him, "Your mother and your brothers and sisters are outside, asking for you." And he replied, "Who are my mother and my brothers?" And looking at those who sat around him, he said, "Here are my mother and my brothers! Whoever does the will of God is my brother and sister and mother."[9]

It's one of the hard things about being faithful: knowing when it's okay and not okay to let people go. We get caught in that bend-back of the roller coaster, where Christian social niceness meets honest-to-Gospel love. I wanted to believe my brother would show up, and I also wanted it to not matter to me.

At my desk in Pennsylvania, still in the process of unpacking boxes, I tried to figure out what to do about the rest of my extended family, and I landed on the idea of a card, a sort of Valentine's-time-frame address-change Christmas-card substitute. I put it on nice recycled stock, the kind of paper that feels substantial in your hand. I learned all about good stationery from my mother. She kept hers organized in boxes in the drawers of her desk—this box for replying to invitations, that box for condolence notes, lovely cards from a museum, and monogrammed sheets for personal correspondence. Everything was arranged so neatly. Sometimes I got to sit at her desk and write a note, like a real lady. Now that desk, one of the many things my brother and I divvied up after our father died, sits in his house. A woman who does not consider me an equal human being has the use of it.

---

[9] Mark 3:31–35.

Some portion of the people who received our announcement had similar feelings. The older generation of my mother's family never communicated with me again. My mother's best friend from childhood wrote me a strong letter about my poor judgment and my bad marriages. Maybe it shouldn't have surprised me that the people who expressed the least interest in my inner workings were the most put off by knowing something true about me.

I've seen my brother once since then, but the kind of communications we had over some family funerals left me feeling there was nothing much more to say. When I learned that cousin reunions were being held and I was not among those being included, though I live much closer now, it hurt—especially the first time. I ached that all these people didn't know, or want to know, me or my family.

Not okay! Not okay!

I tend to think I take other people's feelings into account more often than they do mine, and for that I will also take my share of the responsibility. Maybe a photo card wasn't the kindest way to come out to my Christmas card list. Maybe the older generation minded the number of my marriages as much as the gender of the partner. Yet there had always been something about me that did not match their expectations for a family member. I was fat. I married a Yankee. I moved away. I didn't call enough. I was extravagant with long distance if I called. I lived too far away for too long. We didn't know each other any more, one told me, as if we ever really had.

Okay. Okay, okay, okay, okay, okay.

What do we do about the people who are part of our family of origin, but not part of our family of heart? I know how many times Jesus tells us to forgive, and I'm aware that he wants us to love and pray for our enemies, but he also encourages us to be clear about what family really is. No one could shame him into going out to lunch with his people when they arrived to carry him off and spare themselves the embarrassment of his radical lifestyle. He expressed a sort of gentle surprise at the idea anyone would expect him to leap up and reunite with that crowd from Nazareth. He was doing his work and doing it God's way.

It may hurt your feelings if you prefer other versions of Jesus's story, where he makes sure to arrange a place for mom, but Mark's gospel is helpful to me. There is a difference between loving people with kindness and generosity and the detached humor Jesus practices, and making yourself the landing zone for hurt you know will keep coming. Some people can't and won't understand who you are or what you're doing. Look at the religious authorities. Look at his family. They didn't try to know Jesus; they surely wouldn't go to the trouble for ordinary mortals.

I'm trying to cultivate that bemused frankness I believe Jesus shared with the people closest to him. "You are my family," he told them, "this group I have gathered around me." He told them that just after he called them on the mountain. "You take the place of my brothers and sisters and mother." I have my family of heart: my wife and our children and more. When I saw the Facebook pictures of this year's gathering of "all the cousins," I knew I needed to forgive them. I hoped they would forgive me. Then I let them go.

And it was okay.

Love at a Funeral

Rachel

G iven the choice between officiating a funeral or a wedding, I'd choose a funeral every time. It's a little morbid, perhaps, but most clergy I know prefer funerals to weddings, as I do, although we each have our own reasons. Some ministers want nothing to do with wedding planners and bridezillas (or groomzillas, because that happens too). Some have an intense distaste for the perfumed romanticism that drips over and obscures worship in a wedding ceremony. Some of my colleagues find funerals simpler: no white runners to lay down the center aisle, no flower petals and rice littering the church carpet, no expectations that the ceremony must be perfect to fulfill the couple's lifelong dreams for one perfect day.

Personally, I prefer funerals because of the ways love shows up: raw and vulnerable and choked up, with tears and a dripping nose, not hidden behind veils, not floating on the strains of a processional march. Love at a funeral is love in grief, it's love in thanksgiving, it's even love in anger, all of which are difficult to hide behind flowers and matching outfits. At a funeral, love shows up with experience. At a wedding, love shows up with jewelry. At a funeral, love's commitment tells its stories. At a wedding, love's commitment puts on performances—cake cutting and bouquet tossing and garter removing and sand pouring and many other far more meaningful traditions. When I preside at a funeral, I say God's love can never be deterred, not even by death. When I conduct a wedding, the couple says their love will never be deterred, although, invariably, it will be.

Funerals, at least in my tradition, aren't camera-ready occasions. We don't take turns posing alongside the casket; we don't pause for selfies next to the headstone. Notice the lack of reality television shows about eulogy competitions, or casket buying, or church ladies who put out the best funeral spreads. Meanwhile there is an abundance of programming about dress shopping in bridal salons, competitions for the best weddings, poorly-behaving brides, green-card weddings, cake baking, and unique wedding traditions. Even when Jesus attended a wedding, the focus was on the perfect execution of details—in particular, wine availability and quality: the crisis of wine shortage and Jesus's miraculous restocking of the host's supply. But what do we really learn about love from a miracle of alcohol? How did the attendees know the couple's love better—or how do we know God's love better—because the wedding overflowed with good wine at the end of the party and not just at its beginning?

But give me "Jesus wept,"[1] and I can tell you immediately about Jesus's love poured out in grief for Lazarus, and I can tell you about God's weeping love for the cries of humanity. Give me a stone-faced widower who refuses to shed a tear for fear of falling apart in public, and I can tell you about a trembling love strong enough to move mountains. Give me the anger of a child over a deceased parent's misdeeds, or the rage of a parent at God for a child who dies young, and I can tell you of love's ferocity. Give me a crowd of mourners or just one who shows up to bear witness to life's end, and I can tell you of love's faithfulness. Love's depth and drive are on full display in times of death. Although at weddings we say, "Love conquers all," at funerals we're forced to examine whether we believe it, and we lean on all of Scripture for the affirmation of God's grace showing up in the shit of life, in the valleys of bones, on the hills of crucifixion.

To be sure, the love of engaged couples can inspire and uplift our spirits, too: the once-bitten-twice-shy couple who believe that love has called them to try again in a second or third marriage; the young lovers who have not yet known life's worst, trusting they will

---

[1] John 11:35, KJV.

be stronger together when such moments come; the heart-pounding thrill of wedding vows that will be impossible to keep, though we believe ourselves heroic enough to try. Such love can indeed reflect God—and I consider it an honor to support couples in celebrating such a moment—but the ceremony itself rarely calls our hearts toward God in a way that takes center stage over all the decorations. There is a prayer here and there at weddings, some religious symbolism, even the rites and sacraments, but still the occasion shouts, "Look at the couple," more than, "Look at God." At a wedding, the couple's love is the good news of the day. At a funeral, there simply is no good news except God—all else is death that has provoked love to grieve.

> More love.
> Like rain for the desert: more love.
> Like salve for the wounded: more love.
> We are thirsting
> and hurting.
> More love, O God.
> Love to wash away the fear
> that hides behind our eyes;
> Love to dissolve the doubt
> that lodges itself in our hearts;
> Love to break down the walls
> that prevent hands from holding
> and from being held.[2]

It's worth noting that I've attended, not just officiated, some really great weddings, and I've spent my share of time gladly fussing over wedding details, including the details of dresses. The first dress I remember wearing to a wedding was a pink dream, with ruffles at the shoulders and along the neckline, a layered floor-length skirt, and a thin silky ribbon that tied at the waist. I was six, or maybe five—young enough to be adorable—and a flower girl alongside my

---

[2] Rachel G. Hackenberg, excerpt of "More Love," December 6, 2016, rachelhackenberg.com.

older sister, who wore an identical dress in blue, at the wedding of a woman whose name I don't remember. My sister and I carried plastic pink and blue bouquets. The only other memory I have of that wedding was the couple's first dance to Anne Murray's "Could I Have This Dance," thus securing its place in my memory as the most romantic song ever because I was six and I was in pink and I felt glorious.

I wasn't in a wedding again until my own wedding many years later. My dress was a simple off-white A-line, no train, with a wintery sheen to suit the November event. I wore a veil attached to a silver headband, and pearl-colored shoes that we found on clearance. It was when I knelt for the pastor's blessing during the ceremony that I suddenly panicked and prayed my shoes did not still have the bright orange "discount" stickers on the bottoms that were facing the congregation. Thankfully, the stickers were not there. In hindsight, I should have spent that time praying for the marriage itself.

Periwinkle was the color of choice for the wedding party at my older sister's ceremony, a mere month after my second child was born. This time my self-image was a far cry from a confident six-year-old's glory. My post-pregnant, regularly-nursing body was crammed and literally pinned into periwinkle, struggling to feel pretty and look poised for the day. Orchid was chosen for the bridesmaids' attire when my younger sister married. This time there was no excuse for the extra weight and fatigue and disastrous last-minute haircut, but some advances in undergarment technology and a little makeup and wine helped my self-image assemble itself reasonably well. Both ceremonies for my sisters' marriages were beautiful. The flowers and décor were gorgeous, the music was lively, and everyone was dressed to impress.

In contrast, I have no idea what I wore when my maternal grandmother died, though the funeral was not even a year ago, but I clearly recall my uncle's eulogy reminding us that Grandma's love for her family was a glimpse of heaven. Likewise I couldn't tell you what I wore to the burial of my paternal grandfather ten years ago, but the echoes of the twenty-one gun salute still ring in my ears and

I will always remember the pastor comparing a story of Grandpa chasing a loose steer through the suburbs to Psalm 23 and God's determined care for us as the Great Shepherd. For all of the thought and planning that goes into weddings, I'd rather remember these funeral stories of love than the colors of wedding dresses.

It makes me wonder if we—the Church through generations—have gotten it wrong all these years in remembering Jesus's miracle at the wedding in Cana. We've put a nice theological spin on it, to be sure. We study what the miracle tells us about Jesus's relationship with his mother Mary the God-bearer. We preach on the importance of everyday kindnesses as simple as a glass of good wine. We liken the story to the parable of the last being first. But maybe the wedding at Cana is just a reflection of our oh-so-human habit of fixating on the irrelevant: dress colors and cake decorations and wine quality. Like the arguments in church about carpet colors. Like the disputes between newlyweds over household chores. Like the fascination with fantasy sports leagues. Like beating my own high scores on my phone's apps. We notoriously elevate the immaterial to great significance, and we denigrate or dismiss what is truly important. Of what concern to Jesus was wine at a wedding?[3]

Of what concern to Jesus was the death of a friend? Scripture doesn't record the gifts of food brought to Mary and Martha's home while they observed a time of mourning after their brother's death, although surely food was brought. No one made a note of whether there was enough wine for the mourners, or whether its quality was sufficient for the occasion. In times of death, many details are attended to carefully, necessarily, lovingly, but they are not the details we remember. Instead, those who remembered the occasion of Lazarus's death wrote down the details of Jesus's relationship with Mary and Martha: how they asked for his presence when Lazarus was dying, how the sisters trusted the promises of Jesus as Messiah but openly shared their grief with him, how Jesus was moved to tears to see Mary cry and to visit the place of Lazarus's burial, how Jesus

---

[3] John 2:4.

loved them all so much that he withstood the smell of a four-days-gone dead body, how the resurrected Lazarus had to be unwrapped from all the adornments of burial.

This is what it looks like to celebrate love at a funeral: It's weepy and smelly (not always literally); there are stories and tensions and commiseration. Somehow Paul missed the messiness of love when he penned those verses so often quoted at weddings: "Love is patient; love is kind."[4] Many days—not only on the occasions of funerals and weddings—I'd like to see us celebrate a more candid kind of love:

> Love does not beat around the bush.
> Love tells you when you messed up.
> Love is jealous, not for its own sake,
>   but for others' sake.
> Love ugly-cries.
> Love has lost its patience with hatred.
> Love hopes, but it doesn't put all of its
>   eggs in one basket.
> Love believes you should call more often.
> Love doesn't give gifts; it shows up.
> Love has faith and humility, but it keeps
>   good boundaries.
> Love gets mad when it goes wrong.
> Love does not tolerate b.s.
> Love gets lost.
> Love laughs so hard it pees its pants a little.

Maybe Jesus said all these things when he toasted the couple at the wedding in Cana. Maybe he incorporated it into his prayer at Lazarus's tomb, too.

"God Almighty, I know you hear me when I say this man's death stinks. I'm saying it out loud because the crowd has already seen me ugly cry. I should have shown up sooner, but relationships are

---

[4] 1 Corinthians 13:4.

complicated and I didn't want even my closest friends to think that I'm Messiah-On-Demand, so I took my time. Now, by your power, I reveal death for the b.s. that it truly is: Lazarus, come out!" Maybe that's not what Jesus said. But maybe there's some truth here, not in the bizarre speech but in the radical miracle of love showing up with all its messiness and pouring itself out in recognition of death. Lazarus was raised back to life—not our usual experience of funerals. But it's miraculous how love transforms us when death happens. Sometimes the transformation is a comforted heart when it feels like the loss should break us completely. Sometimes the transformation is a released heart when contortions of love have dominated our lives. Like water transformed into wine, love pours over death to transform the continuation of life. Why waste such a miracle on weddings? Jesus changing water to wine at a funeral would have made much more sense to me.

When I got married, the wedding was planned on a dime, compared to the financial expectations of the modern wedding industry. My dress came from a department store's racks of winter formals, and we were still trimming my tulle veil moments before the ceremony. The invitations were printed at home, the maroon ribbons were hand-tied to the small wedding bells everyone rang after our church ceremony. The hall of the Lion's Club served as the reception space. Except for a small wedding cake topped with a plastic lily, all of the reception food was homemade. It was a modest gathering that was rich in community; no one sat alone or off to the side. Everyone mingled and talked and laughed and danced.

If water had turned to wine on that November night, people would still be talking about my wedding today, almost twenty years later. It would have been the one thing remembered from the occasion, not because the event wasn't great on its own merits, but because such a miracle would have given everyone a common story. The love between two people at a wedding does not always become the shared story of the gathered community, even though it is the center of attention for the event. But when someone dies, those who show up share a grief borne of a common love. No one's love for that person is centered to the detriment or dismissal of the others' love for the deceased. Gathered in hospice or in church or at a funeral parlor or at the graveside, love has company. With any luck, it also has good wine.

Did He See the Angel That Caught Him?

Martha

The ring of my cell phone woke me from a deep sleep in the first hour of a summer Thursday. I fumbled for the phone on my bedside table, recognized the Michigan area code, and answered reflexively.

"Mom." It was my son Peter's familiar voice. "Mom, I'm okay."

Now I was awake. The story unfolded in disjointed fragments. He was calling from an emergency room near Grand Rapids. He had been declared bruised but unbroken after being thrown from a convertible driven by the friend who picked him up at the airport. Suitcases and wallets had flown out of the open car, eyeglasses, cell phones, a clarinet, and a cello. My boy had flown with them, hurtled out of the car.

In shock, and cared for by a nurse who happened upon the scene and bundled him in blankets, he had made the journey via ambulance to the emergency room, where the medical staff had checked him for every kind of injury: broken this and lacerated that, internal injuries, and external disasters. The medical staff then let him make a phone call, after x-rays and a CT scan determined he had no internal bleeding, only "serious" bruising on his chest and legs.

He tried to reassure me. The driver had climbed out and walked away; the other passenger had required stitches in one of his two cut knees. His friends said that, even dirty and bruised, his stand-up hairstyle still looked great. He had to hang up to get his discharge instructions. When he called back to tell me a friend's mom was going to take them all in for what remained of the night, he sounded subdued, and less intent on comforting me.

"Mom," he said, "I thought I was going to die."

Peter is my second child, and the one who left home at the youngest age. He went to the Interlochen Arts Academy, near the pinky finger of the mitten part of Michigan, to study clarinet for his last two years of high school. Now in college, he was traveling to work on the stage crew for the Interlochen summer camp and concert series. At nineteen, a road trip with friends seems like the obvious way to travel. The young driver had a new car; he picked up one friend along the way, and then they met Peter at the airport in Grand Rapids. They found a place to have dinner, and that should have been their last stop before arriving at Interlochen. They packed the little red BMW convertible, top down, full of all their luggage for camp, plus golf clubs. A cello in its impressively fashioned protective case rode in the backseat like a passenger. In the pale light of a long summer evening, Peter wedged in among the suitcases with his bag and his clarinet case.

At home in Maine, I thought I might hear from him as he and his friends drove to Interlochen. I called his number several times, leaving only one brief message. Peter and Edward had often compared me to the overreacting mother in the semi-famous headline from *The Onion*, "Area Mom Freaking Out For No Reason Again." I didn't want to be that mom. I stayed up a little later than usual, but finally convinced myself that he had forgotten to turn his phone on after landing, or just didn't put his mother that high on the list of priorities. His phone had been thrown out of the car with everything else; it was never found.

The next morning I called all the people who mattered, who needed to know, or who I knew I could lean on in that liminal moment when the threshold between the best news and the worst seemed precariously narrow. Kathryn, best of all friends, asked, "Did he see the angel that caught him?"

In general, I have trouble with theology that says God purposely protects this person or that one, because it suggests a cavalier attitude on the part of the Divine toward many other people not encased in metaphysical bubble wrap. But for that day, and for some time to come, I felt grateful for God's protection. For that day, I believed in miracles, in an angel who pulled a young man in one direction while a car flipped the other, in a savior who happened to be walking through town just in time to bring a young man back from the dead before the people could bury him.

> Soon afterwards [Jesus] went to a town called Nain, and his disciples and a large crowd went with him. As he approached the gate of the town, a man who had died was being carried out. He was his mother's only son, and she was a widow; and with her was a large crowd from the town. When the Lord saw her, he had compassion for her and said to her, "Do not weep." Then he came forward and touched the bier, and the bearers stood still. And he said, "Young man, I say to you, rise!" The dead man sat up and began to speak, and Jesus gave him to his mother. Fear seized all of them; and they glorified God, saying, "A great prophet has risen among us!" and "God has looked favorably on his people!" This word about him spread throughout Judea and all the surrounding country.[5]

There's nothing like raising someone from the dead to get everyone's attention.

---

[5] Luke 7:11–17.

Jesus brought some young person back to life in each of the gospels. Mark and Matthew tell the story of Jairus's young daughter; John offers the long narrative of Lazarus's death and reanimation. Each of the stories makes it clear: God has power over death, power to restore life where we cannot believe it will come again. The widow in Luke's gospel was weeping over her only son, as she would in any time and place. In her religious tradition, a burial took place within twenty-four hours of death. The wound was deep, and it was fresh. The only son of a widow meant more than a beloved daughter or brother. A widow was already among the people in need of special care, and an only son was the last person who had the responsibility to look out for her.

The entire Gospel of Luke proclaims God's urgent concern for all people who are at such risk. Mary sang of it in the Magnificat. Jesus preached his first sermon at the synagogue in Nazareth in response to the story of Elijah's giving aid to a widow. He never stopped pressing the religious authorities on their responsibilities to the disadvantaged. In chapter 7, Jesus not only showed that God had power over death but that God was willing to use it, even inclined to use it, to help the people least able to help themselves.

On that first day after the accident, I hated to leave Lucy and go to work. Her presence, alive and precious, brought up tears I hid from everyone else. I tried to figure out whether or not to get on a plane to Michigan. Peter was bruised, and he needed to elevate his calves, but otherwise his instructions were simply to rest and take pain medication as needed. I wanted to go, but what exactly would I do? His dad downplayed the need. So did my boss. We had an important meeting that night, and as far as he was concerned, the news was good.

The mom who took Peter in loved interacting with her daughter's friends and assured me over and over that if his needs proved more than she could manage, she would let me know. On that first day, the mom and I spoke often, and, when the pain meds made Peter lethargic, we set a timeline for taking him back to the ER if he didn't rouse more fully. He woke up in plenty of time, sore and hungry. I arranged a time to Skype with him the next day, and I went to sleep on Thursday night searching for a way to describe the past twenty-four hours. Blessed felt like too arrogant a word to use, lucky too fatalistic, and surreal a bit ungrateful.

Friday morning I turned on the television while making coffee and heard someone else's surreal, unblessed, bad luck news. A sixteen-year-old boy from Portland High School had flipped his car. The convertible Peter was in had turned over two-and-a-half times; he flew out on the first rotation. The Portland boy was driving an SUV. The news didn't say how many times it went over. They only said he was dead. Peter was not dead. Lucy soon heard that the dead boy was someone from her gym class, a year ahead of her, and by the end of the day I knew he was related to a colleague of mine, and had been on the way home from visiting his girlfriend in another town. The driver of the convertible had swerved to avoid a deer; the boy from Lucy's school was going too fast around a curve. Both accidents were attributed to driver inexperience.

My family huddled around a laptop that afternoon to see Peter's face. Edward, out of college and living in New York City, happened to be passing through town that day. We didn't ask too many questions in that first conversation, and I later learned that some answers Peter couldn't have given and some he just wouldn't, not yet. I didn't say much because all I wanted to say felt unspeakable. "Thank God you are alive. I don't know why you are alive, but thank God for it." Edward and Lucy received an unreasonable number of proxy hugs. Somewhere else in town a family huddled together at a funeral home, making unthinkable arrangements.

That Friday was beautiful, the kind of day that makes living through the hard seasons in Maine worthwhile. We took a walk on a path by a marsh. Along the way we found an installation of sculptures made from twisted metal. In Michigan, the convertible driver and the other passenger went to the car yard to retrieve whatever belongings had been towed along with the car. They took pictures of what was left of it. Somewhere in some other salvage yard sat the

SUV. What could that other family possibly find in it that would matter?

When Lucy first told me the name of the boy in the SUV, I remembered he was the kid who had picked on her in their gym class. He had insulted her for being the slowest runner, for being generally clumsy, for maybe being gay because she walked laps with the same friend every day. There are some theologies, some ways of understanding God, that might give us permission to think he was being punished in that accident, or that family sins had been visited on him, or that God simply keeps God's hands off our free will, including driver inexperience. There are some, even worse, that lead people to tell the grieving mother of a boy who dies in a car accident that God must have needed him more in heaven than we needed him here. That's the worst. Don't ever say that to anyone.

Lucy and I sat uncomfortably with her memories of gym class. His death felt closer to us than it would have otherwise. It felt wrong to celebrate what had happened to us knowing another family was suffering. A few days later we read her classmate's obituary in the newspaper. His family history resembled ours. He went to church. He participated in youth group. His pastor called him kind. I thought of his mother and felt some mixture of guilt, relief, and grief.

Peter began to feel better. He watched a lot of videos that first weekend, whole seasons of *30 Rock*. Before he moved to his summer housing the following week, we had one more long Skype conversation. He focused on the weird things about the accident he had not told me before. He wasn't wearing a seat belt. It was the first time in his life he had not. The car was so full, it seemed unnecessary jammed into the back seat. That was why he sailed out as soon as the car left the ground. The taller of the two boys who flipped with the car felt his head touch the ground twice as it went over. The roll bar saved them.

Whoa. That felt too heavy. Peter would not, could not, speak of the nearness of death. He lightened the conversation with another amazing fact, this one about their musical instruments. The clarinet was fine, and, when its case was opened, the cello proved to be in tune. We joked that they should offer testimonials to the manufacturer. I asked if he wanted to come home. I asked more than once in those first few days, not to press him, but to let him know that I cared more about how he felt, physically and emotionally, than whether he earned money at a summer job. I tried to say the right things, to create the right openings, to respect the right moments of silence. I tried not to freak out again for no reason. I tried to put my gratitude for his life into words without sounding saccharine or smug or set apart. My son was alive, and someone else's was dead. I could not make sense of it.

In August, he got a ride back to Maine with a brother and sister he met at the camp. Their plans seemed indefinite, the itinerary uncertain, the timing less than precise. I waited with an eye on the driveway for the better part of a day until a little Toyota pulled in and Peter got out. His clothes were packed in a collapsible laundry hamper. I had forgotten that his suitcase did not fare as well as his clarinet case. I hugged him gingerly, as if the accident had been the day before instead of eight weeks earlier.

> The dead man sat up and began to speak, and
> Jesus gave him to his mother.[6]

On another gorgeous Maine summer evening, we sat on the terrace at our favorite sushi place, and heard more pieces of the story. He told us about the nurse who pulled over behind them and found broken bottles in the back of the car; she wanted to hide them before the police got there, to help the young driver, but he assured her it was special root beer from his home town. He had packed a case to bring to camp. We all laughed in the face of death and the authorities. These boys were somehow protected, but by fate? by stupidity? by that angel? The nurse thought they would all be dead. I

---

[6] Luke 7:15.

stayed angry for a long time with the parents who thought it was a good idea to give their nineteen-year-old a red BMW convertible.

Peter told us there were pictures of the car and asked if I wanted to see them. I waited longer, I think until Christmas vacation. First, I looked at the before shots—the little car full of suitcases, the golf clubs wedged just behind the front seats, between Peter and the cello. Now I could see where the roll bar was, where Peter's head was. The golf clubs didn't fall out of the car; their heads snapped off.

There's nothing like raising someone from the dead to get everyone's attention. We don't know what had happened to the widowed mother's only son. Did he have an accident at work, eat some food that had gone bad, or fall victim to a fever? Any resurrection seems unlikely when you know your beloved child is dead, whether you have nursed him faithfully, or heard the bad news in screams coming from the field. I feel angry sometimes that Jesus gave us an explicit hope that so seldom comes to life.

It was another year before Peter told me the driver of the convertible was speeding when he swerved to avoid the deer. It was twilight, and they were all in high spirits, though not under the influence of any. I'm still not sure I know the truth of how fast he was going, but fast enough that the swerving car flipped once, twice, and half again. Hanging upside down, the boys in the front seat crawled out through the broken windshield. I guess they expected to find Peter dead, but instead they found him trying to stand up, even though he was in shock. He fell, and the nurse brought a blanket from her car and wrapped him in it. She wrapped them all in a blanket of protection. If I could talk to anyone about what happened that night, I wish I could talk to her.

We have told the story out loud and in our minds until we can believe it, mostly. How could it be anything but a miracle? Whom could we credit but an angel? And why didn't that other family get one, too?

AFTERWORD

Martha

On the same day that this book's first draft went to the editor, I rode a gurney into an operating room. My failures of faith were very much on my mind, particularly my superpower of denial, my reluctance to pray silently, my questions about why some people always seem to get out alive, my fear of being a mistake, and my attempts to be someone I was not.

I had to leave Kathryn behind in the waiting room for part of the pre-op festivities. A nurse recorded my vital signs. Then I was left to undress, put on those non-skid socks, scrub my belly with some kind of antiseptic wipe for three minutes, timer provided, and put on a hospital gown with the opening in the back. Watching the timer tick down, I could not deny what lay ahead: a laparoscopic surgery that might solve a problem and be the only treatment needed, or that might be only the beginning of bad news and further complications. I pushed my belongings into a green plastic bag and got in the bed to await the IV, the visits from doctors, and the happy sight of my wife finally allowed to join me.

Having decided that denial really didn't give God an opportunity to be in relationship with me, I spent the weeks before the scheduled surgery working on a new prayer practice. I particularly sought one that did not rely entirely on my words. It had been helpful to read Rachel's chapters, in part because our childhood faith communities taught us to relate to God differently. Southern Baptists, the tribe of my youth, emphasized the personal relationship with the One, even if such intimacy meant an uncomfortable awareness of how much that One knows about who you are and what you do. When I grew up and joined a historically Congregational United Church of Christ congregation in Maine, I discovered a more corporate sense of God's presence and action—God in relationship to the gathered body and to the world. The Congregational God didn't square with the intimate parental figure I had been taught to revere. The Congregational God allowed us more room to figure things out, expected us to take more responsibility, and was not a Divine Micromanager.

I want to think there is some way to hold both of these views of God as true. I especially wanted it in the weeks between the day I learned I needed surgery and the day I went to the hospital. What could I do, I asked myself, that would help me to be ready no matter the outcome? I had just returned from a conference where the presenters recommended the practice of centering prayer. The suggestion felt like it was directed at me, with my secret history of contemplative failures. In a gentle tone, one of the speakers asked all of us, "If you knew God was going to show up and sit next to you at a particular time every day, wouldn't you make sure to be there?" Challenge accepted.

I sat every day for a week, using the Insight Timer app on my iPhone—because who doesn't love a graph of how often they have prayed and for how long? I lengthened the time each day, and each day I remonstrated with myself for not being better at emptying my mind, focusing on my breath, and letting stray thoughts pass out of my consciousness. Thanks be to God I had an appointment with my therapist, Kim, that week. When I told her my problem, she laughed gently.

"You don't actually expect to master something immediately, do you?"

Expect? No. Desire? Yes. Time felt short.

On my therapist's advice, I went back to the Insight Timer and found some guided contemplative prayers. There was a human voice for part of each session, but at least it wasn't mine. I smiled when Buddhist practitioner Jack Kornfield's famously soothing voice reminded listeners that learning to meditate is like training a puppy. You repeat the commands and put the puppy back in position as many times as needed. "Be gentle," he said. "There's no need to beat the puppy."

Gently and gingerly, I sat again each morning, no longer expecting or fearing some kind of divine proclamation on my worthiness or lack thereof, but feeling better-resourced for whatever might come next. It turns out I was right when I wrote months ago that a two-way relationship with God is the point of prayer.

I made conversation as the nurse pushed me on the gurney to the brightly lit operating room. I noted the tables of covered surgical instruments and the neatly packaged surgical drapes that would be used to cover me. I could not deny them. As I lay there, I was not a pastor or a writer or a wife or a mother or a queer or a failure. None of that mattered. I was there, and it was happening, and I did not feel alone in it.

"I'm going to give you something to relax you," said my new best friend, the anesthesiologist. Two hours later I woke up in recovery, trying to guess by the clock what the outcome might be.

The news was good. After a quick "Thanks be to God," Kathryn and I turned our attention to things like what kind of pain medicine I would be taking, and what I could eat and drink, and how soon a room would be available. Kathryn was on her phone to send messages to our kids, and began hearing bad news from members of the church she serves: another person having surgery the same day whose outcome was not so positive, and a couple whose fifty-five-year-old son had been found dead that morning.

Even when we are celebrating, someone else is suffering.

I came home with discharge instructions, prescription pain meds, and hospital ice packs. I'll admit to being a bit shocked that I remained in a condition that prevented me from being anything to anybody. You know you're in a bad way when laughing hurts. Kathryn washed my hair and helped me dress. I needed help to get from our high bed to a stool and then the floor. Each time I rolled over gingerly and maneuvered my legs over the side, then pushed up on an elbow, I needed her close by. After my feet touched down,

I rested my arm on her shoulders as I stood. Our cheeks brushed gently, and each time she whispered, "This is my favorite part." I imagine that would have been true even if the news had been bad. Maybe especially if the news had been bad.

It feels just that good to be close to God in the day to day, a cheek's brush distance: sitting, listening, getting distracted, and beginning again. I expect more failures of faith in my future. I expect to keep asking questions without answers, struggling to get through meditations, counting on people for things they cannot give. I can only keep trying to be the person God made me to be.

Gently, then, gingerly, I hope to get better with practice. I hope the same for you.

Rachel

Shortly before my then-husband's criminal trial, I called a friend and mentor to tell her the news. She offered a listening ear and prayers, and then she said,

"This is what the resurrection is about." She repeated it. "This is what the resurrection is about. You'll be a better preacher and pastor because you've had this experience of resurrection."

She didn't mean that the trial would be a resurrection experience—trust me, it wasn't. She meant that resurrection only comes after the catastrophe of death, after the chaos of endings, after the explosion of our worlds' bubbles. She meant that resurrection is not only an other-worldly dream that we wait to realize in the by-and-by but a tangible, lived experience in this world too. She meant that ministry must recognize the valley of the shadow of death in everyday life so that it can also testify to the green pastures that are new every morning.

I understood what she meant. Since that conversation, a conviction for this world's resurrections has shaped my ministry. But all these years later, I struggle to live toward my own mind-body-spirit resurrection in Christ. My mind tries to obtain its own resurrection through excellence. My body has placed its trust for resurrection in denial. My spirit is chasing resurrection to the bottom of every cup of chai.

Resurrection: I suppose it's yet another failure of faith to add to the list.

Nevertheless, writing out these stories of failure has been an effort to practice the resurrection that I preach, to look candidly at life's sins and griefs and cynicisms, and to hear within it all God's unexpected story of life instead of replaying my own spirit's familiar story of defect and devastation. For some of *Denial's* stories, resurrection means laughing at myself like Sarah laughed at her body's age when God promised to do a new thing. God took a little girl who ordered toys in the church nursery and gave her a church order to love. I'm telling you, loving church order is a very peculiar calling in life; God and I are still actively debating and laughing over this one. For some of *Denial's* stories, practicing resurrection means practicing confession. Peter confessed Jesus as Lord over a hot fish breakfast on the beach, and I confess God as Sovereign every time a cup of caffeine doesn't guarantee a manageable day.

There are stories in *Denial* still awaiting resurrection. Who knows how God will make use of a particular turn of events or of me. The post-traumatic stress disorder diagnosis was a new discovery that unfolded during the same timeframe that Martha and I were writing this book. For every diagnosis we receive, for every new season in life we enter, for every shift in our relationships and circumstances, we modify our perspectives on life and faith. We pay attention to God differently. We relate to one another and to ourselves differently. All of these shifts hold possibilities for resurrection, too. Of course, it should be named that some of our failures will not be resurrected at all until that glorious day when the lion lies down with the lamb. That's why we celebrate Advent, that's why we have something called apocalyptic eschatology—the wild and radical claim that God's salvation in the final days makes a difference for us today.

Writing down the unresolved failures in particular has reminded me that I preach a God who is able to craft unexpected endings—nothing fairy-tale or fantastical, or maybe entirely fairy-tale and fantastical—but most of all something different than the dismal ending I had assumed. Perhaps an awareness of pain again, so that it can be felt and healed. Perhaps a fresh practice of prayer that helps me dust off my words from their weariness. Perhaps an introduction to a new caffeinated beverage; it's a low bar, but I'd consider it a reasonable starting point toward change. To be sure, writing down stories of failure—even in pursuit of resurrection—still feels like airing dirty laundry to me, which I would much rather do in the privacy of a backyard clothesline than a published book. But Martha and I started this project because we saw ourselves in each other's life stories, as though we were neighbors hanging out laundry on the same day and noticing across the backyard fence that we both had grass-stained jeans on the line, or as though we were holding up mirrors to one another and noticing common features: You wear glasses too? You ignore your body's pain levels too? You're completely skeptical of certain spiritual practices too?

Our best hope is not that you read these stories and say, "Wow, cool dirty laundry," but that you find a mirror for your spirit somewhere within these pages, a glimmer of a reflection to assure you that you're not alone—in faith or in life, in pain or in change—and that you recognize yourself within God's broader story. We hope that you take your insights to a neighbor or a friend who's also trying to wrangle their dirty laundry, that you commiserate over failures and griefs and pains, that you keep each other company through all that remains unresolved. Because that, too, would be a resurrection.

ACKNOWLEDGMENTS

From Martha Spong:

Thank you to all the people who have encouraged me to write: my dear friend and coauthor, Rachel, who thought our voices would go well together; our editor, Milton, who long ago told me to run toward the open space; Karla, who heard my confession; Barbara Melosh, who convinced me to keep at it; Edward, Peter, and Lucy, who let me share family stories both here and in years' worth of sermons, blog posts, and stories; the late addition, Will, who asks all the questions; and my wife, Kathryn, who makes all things possible, from the first cup of coffee to the last out of the game.

From Rachel G. Hackenberg:

This book was Martha's idea; for her friendship and brilliance I am grateful. Milton's editing eye and encouragement have been tremendous gifts in the work of telling hard stories well. I should thank therapists everywhere who do good work in a heartbreaking world. There are pivotal people in my life who are unafraid to love through failure, and while they are too many to name, I'm especially indebted to the ongoing love and presence of Jesse & Diane and Sondra & Dave. In recent years, Eric has kept me praying and Meredith has kept me swearing and both have kept me honest; their friendships have been lifelines of hope more than they know. Noah and Faith are my joy and my sanity—thank you.